All the King's Daughters

BY
CHRISTY ROSE

TRILOGY
A WHOLLY OWNED SUBSIDIARY OF TBN
PROFESSIONAL PUBLISHING MEETS POWERFUL PROMOTION.

All the King's Daughters

Trilogy Christian Publishers A Wholly Owned Subsidiary of Trinity Broadcasting Network

2442 Michelle Drive Tustin, CA 92780

Copyright © 2023 by Christy Rose

Scripture quotations marked NIV are taken from the Holy Bible, New International Version®, NIV®. Copyright © 1973, 1978, 1984, 2011 by Biblica, Inc.™ Used by permission of Zondervan. All rights reserved worldwide. www.zondervan.com. The "NIV" and "New International Version" are trademarks registered in the United States Patent and Trademark Office by Biblica, Inc.™

No part of this book may be reproduced, stored in a retrieval system, or transmitted by any means without written permission from the author. All rights reserved. Printed in the USA.

Rights Department, 2442 Michelle Drive, Tustin, CA 92780.

Trilogy Christian Publishing/TBN and colophon are trademarks of Trinity Broadcasting Network.

Cover image: iStock/Unsplash

For information about special discounts for bulk purchases, please contact Trilogy Christian Publishing.

Trilogy Disclaimer: The views and content expressed in this book are those of the author and may not necessarily reflect the views and doctrine of Trilogy Christian Publishing or the Trinity Broadcasting Network.

10 9 8 7 6 5 4 3 2 1

Library of Congress Cataloging-in-Publication Data is available.

ISBN: 979-8-89041-226-3

E-ISBN: 979-8-89041-227-0

Dedication

I humbly and without hesitation dedicate this book to the ones who make my life fulfilling and complete.

To my precious husband: you show me the love of Jesus every single day, and you lead our family so well. Because you continually remind me of my calling, this book is complete.

To Jack, Ava, and Luke: being your mother is the greatest joy in my life. Because of each of you, I have learned that a broken vessel can still have a purpose greater than itself. I love you endlessly.

Table of Contents

Chapter 1: The Somewhere-In-Between 1

Chapter 2: Rebellious Roots 15

Chapter 3: Beauty for Ashes 32

Chapter 4: Zion 45

Chapter 5: The Mystery Is History! No, Really, It's History .. 56

Chapter 6: The Golden Calf 64

Chapter 7: The Sin We're In: People-Pleasing Edition 83

Chapter 8: Freedom Fighter 100

Chapter 9: The Keys to the Kingdom 134

Chapter 10: Say Whaaattt? 153

CHAPTER 1:
The Somewhere-In-Between

I've always heard the first sentence is the hardest one to write. Thank God that's over.

I'm just a mom, sitting in front of the computer, trying to figure out the best way to tell you how God took the broken little girl from my past and turned her into a victorious, joyful woman who walks in the authority of the Lord. Wow. Feels impossible now that I've typed it out like that, but I can do all things through Christ, right? So, let's jump straight into it. I'm a mom, remember? I don't have all day.

I've been sitting behind the computer screen, pecking away at the keyboard for as long as I can remember. Some kids had a blanket or stuffed animal that brought them comfort, but I have never been like everyone else. I comforted myself by getting lost in my thoughts. When life was a mess and out of my control, I could take words and make the mess feel like a masterpiece. Words have always held power when I have otherwise felt powerless. When I was a small girl, I loved to escape the unfortunate circumstances of my life by creating fictional characters. I could control the beginning, middle, and end of their stories when I couldn't control anything about my own. The ability to do that was more therapeutic than any counseling session I ever went to. When I was a lost teenager hellbent on creating chaos, I could find order and structure within the confines of the lines of college-ruled notebook paper. As a young wife with a husband who deployed oversees during Operation Enduring Freedom and then again in Operation Iraqi Freedom, the only calm I could create within myself was with a journal and pen. My anxiety and tears would fill the absolute depths of my soul until my grieving heart could not put one foot in front of the other. I could only regain strength to move forward by dumping out the fear in my mind onto tear-stained pages of tiny journals. Now, as a mother and wife desperately trying to follow Jesus, God's written word is the only weapon I can count on to defend my family from the relentless attacks of the enemy. My obsession for words, my own and our Creator's, has prepared me for what God has commissioned me to do now in sharing my story with you. As I have prepared to write this book, my prayer is not that I will be filled with good words but rather I be filled with God words.

CHAPTER 1: THE SOMEWHERE-IN-BETWEEN

I believe that God gives each one of us something unique; a talent, a heartache, a heartbreak, something monumental to overcome. Some people can talk and encourage others, but my words come out awkward and ineffective when I try to speak. Others have talent and can sing and play instruments to usher in the presence of the Lord, but that's not me either. My talent lies in the ability to connect with a stranger over words that may never even be spoken out loud. The first time God gave me the desire to write a book was over a decade ago. Since I am just now doing it, I'm sure the truth I'm about to confess to you will come as no surprise. Procrastination has to be in my top five skills of excellence. I've written blogs, I've written daily devotions for my friends on social media, I've written prayers in my journal for only God to see. I'm ashamed to say that even though I knew God gave me a powerful story to tell, I have avoided telling it until now. I can give you a million excuses as to why. I told myself that writing a book wasn't contributing to my family. I considered it a "waste of time" because it didn't produce immediate results. It would require intensive labor, and I didn't think I had extra time to give. I also hid behind the foolish reasoning that since it didn't benefit my family financially, emotionally, or in the very real physical sense like cooking and cleaning does, it was of no purpose. I also knew that telling my truth would expose people I love to unkind memories of the past, and the thought of someone I love being hurt seemed too great a burden to bear. I let the devil feed me lie after lie and was convinced it was my own voice. I danced around obedience but knew in my heart that I was dodging the still, small voice of the Lord. I couldn't reach my destination because I was letting the enemy wear me out before I could even lace up my shoes.

After 2020, I began having the urgency to write and tell others of the hope that I have found in Jesus. The spirit of the Lord rested heavily on me, and I began to see people like I had never seen them before. Maybe it was the masking; maybe it was the fear that we all seemed to share about the unknown. Whatever it was, something caused me to start really looking at people. And everywhere I looked, I saw empty eyes looking back at me. God began to let me see the hurt that others carry and so carefully hide. No matter where I turned, I saw hurting people who desperately needed hope. People needed God to give them beauty for ashes and peace that passes understanding. Since I know what it's like to be the one longing for peace and searching for hope, and God has graciously given it to me, I knew I had to share my message with anyone who would listen. So here I am, looking at the floor that needs to be mopped, the dishes that need to be put away, and the random pop cans scattered around my living room floor practically begging to be thrown away. The urge to tend to the mess is real, but so is the conviction of God. I have a story to tell, so sit down, get comfy, and let the Lord encourage your heart.

About a month ago, I was sitting in church listening to a sermon, and my preacher was on fire! I was taking notes, shouting "amen" every few minutes whilst also still managing to keep my kid's behavior in check with the ever so subtle but wholly terrifying mom glare. I was multitasking like, well, a mother. Of all the things I expected to come from the service that day, I wasn't expecting God to drop a book title in my spirit, but that's exactly what He did. God loves to catch me by surprise! God has been dealing with me for a long time, and He knew if He didn't drop it like it's hot, loud, and clear, almost audibly in my brain, I'd miss it. To be honest, I hadn't thought about writing a book in a very long time. I was so afraid of failing that I failed to do anything at all. The trouble with procrastination is the longer you put it off, the more of a mountain it becomes. When I would come under conviction to write, I'd deploy my best avoidance skills until the feeling passed. And let me just tell you, when I put my mind to something, I always go all in. I would feel God nudge me to write, and suddenly, my to-do list was a mile long. I would find the energy to put away that pile of laundry that had been accumulating for days. I'd deep clean the stove and the microwave. I'd throw away all the old food in the fridge. If I did write, I'd make a devotional post on social media instead. There was always something to fill my mind and my time. Isn't that like the devil to steal our time under the guise of something that seems significant? If he can't make you bad, he'll sure make you busy. I avoided writing until one day, when I wanted to write again, I couldn't think of anything at all. I had writer's block, and it lasted an extended period of time. I just knew that since I refused to obey and wasn't being a good steward of the gift He had given me, He had let me have my way, and I wouldn't have to write at all. Except writing was all I had ever wanted to do, so I was in quite the predicament. Fear struck my heart, but fear is a liar; can I get an amen? I did all I knew to do. I asked for forgiveness for neglecting the good gift He had given me and for my stubborn disobedience. I prayed that He would restore my ability to write His words, His message, and for His purposes. I truly sought His face. God, in His goodness and grace, restored my creativity and gave me the title All the King's Daughters sitting right there in the pew.

I loved the way the title rolled off my tongue. It represented all the women in God's kingdom, not just the ones like me. Mothers, widows, working women, teenagers, single women, engaged women, wives, sisters, daughters. Ones with tattoos and ones without. Piercings, no piercings. Purple and blue hair and the ones who let nature take its course. The list could go on and on. The message I was to deliver was to be for us all. I began praying and pondering what I could offer all women that would be our common ground. Finally, I realized that what I have to offer, what we all have to offer each other, is the truth. My truth is a story of a woman who was so radically transformed by the gospel of Jesus Christ that my core beliefs and character were permanently changed. My wounds were revealed and then graciously healed by the one who loves me more than I could conceivably imagine. The great news is that what He has done for me, He will do for you, too. No one has to live unsatisfied, depressing lives where joy is hard to find and even harder to keep. Throughout this book, I will take you on the winding path that led to righteousness and victory and encourage you to travel the road to righteousness for yourself as well.

I want to take you on a journey with me as I use my own life as an example of how the power of God can transform the most desperately broken woman and transform her into something beautiful. I don't recognize the woman I am about to describe to you anymore, but her memory lives within my heart as a powerful reminder of God's goodness and grace. Without further ado, let me introduce you to a ghost from my past.

Several years ago, I found myself crying all the time. I had three small children, a wonderful husband that worked so hard to provide a great life for us, and a full-time job teaching elementary school. I should have been overjoyed at the life the Lord had blessed me with. Instead of joy, I was constantly drowning in tears. One afternoon is etched in my mind forever. I found myself sitting in the parking lot of my school, staring in the rearview at my blue-eyed kindergartener. He was falling asleep sitting straight up, and on either side of him were two empty car seats that would soon be filled by brother and sister. Grief swept over me, and small, silent tears turned into giant shoulder-shaking sobs. Moments earlier, I had snapped at my sweet boy over something silly, and I could immediately see the hurt and shock in his small face. I was tired. I had been overworked at school and dealt with more than my share of

CHAPTER 1: THE SOMEWHERE-IN-BETWEEN

trouble that day. He didn't deserve the worst part of me, but that sure was what he got. In fact, my family got the worst of me almost every day. I would go into my classroom and give the very best I had to give until my cup was completely empty. And as we all know, you can't pour from an empty cup. I cried myself to sleep that night.

The next day, I was walking around my classroom, unable to contain the emotions that were coming in unexpected waves. My mind was absolutely racing with thoughts until I felt the words literally about to burst from inside my chest. I grabbed a yellow notepad and penned this poem:

THE SOMEWHERE-IN-BETWEEN

I live in the hallelujahs, the sighs, and the somewhere in-betweens,
where love always lives and can be felt,
but occasionally isn't seen.

Where the praises and the struggles
are whispered in the same breath.
Where we are raising three little ones
and it scares us to death.

I live in-between the
"I CAN'T BELIEVE YOU SPILLED JUICE ON THE CARPET
FOR THE THIRD TIME THIS WEEK!"
and the "I'm going to kiss you all over,
you've got sugars dripping off of your cheeks!"

My mind is in a dead sprint
of "Rush, rush, rush, we've got to be fast,"
but my heart says, "Slow down…make these moments last."

I live with self-inflicted noise
that can only be drowned out with prayer,
to my God, who never leaves me and is always right there.

I cry out to Him in whispers, tears, and groans,
He is my faithful rock, never leaving me alone.
Without fail, He calms my often-tormented spirit,
and gently reminds me His voice can be heard
when I'm still enough to hear it.

Give me courage, Lord, to walk away
from the expectations of this life,
and be a godly mother and an ever-present wife.

CHAPTER 1: THE SOMEWHERE-IN-BETWEEN

*I live in the hallelujahs, the sighs, and the somewhere in-betweens,
where I thank God He is my deliverance
and the rock upon which I lean.*

I went home that night, shared my heart with my husband, and we decided the best decision for our family was for me to resign from my teaching position. The trouble with that, of course, was the inability to go from a two-income family to one-income one.

We decided to fast and pray for God to make a way for me to stay home. The days turned into weeks, and on the last day of school, God had yet to fulfill our prayer. I remember walking around my classroom thinking, *Lord, You must want me here. If this is my mission field, I will give it my all.* No sooner than I had spoken to the Lord, my phone rang. It was my husband on the other end. He told me that a small piece of land we had bought and listed for sale several months prior had gotten a full-price offer! After sitting on the market for months with zero interest and then to sell in one day was incredible! But it was what he told me next that made my jaw hit the floor. He had calculated our profit once commission was paid, and it was my salary for the year, almost down to the dollar!!! *God is never late and always right on time!* I went to my computer, typed a resignation letter, and with that, one chapter of my life ended, and another began.

This one answered prayer gave me the courage and faith to step out of the boat and onto the water, and it has made all the difference. Year after year, God has provided. It hasn't always been easy, but He has made provisions time and again. There were times in our journey when I didn't think I would survive the heat from the refining fire. Yet God, in His infinite goodness, has molded and shaped me into something new. With God at the helm, I'd like to pass on my revelations to you.

In Matthew 7:13, God tells us that we should enter through the narrow gate because the gate to destruction is wide and the road is broad. The narrow path can be difficult to see if you don't know what you are looking for. Thankfully, the road that leads to God isn't hidden. A relationship with Him isn't a mystery you have to unlock before you experience. God is clear in His expectations and gives us instruction for every single detail of our lives, every situation, every relationship, every thought, act, and deed. We find ourselves on the broad road, roaming around the wilderness, when we decide to follow our own map over

CHAPTER 1: THE SOMEWHERE-IN-BETWEEN

His. When we find the humility to admit that our ways are not good and ask for His help, He is sure to reveal that narrow gate that leads to Him. It took me much longer than I would like to admit to put my pride aside and ask God to show me the better way.

The roadmap I was following for some time had me walking into all kinds of danger, and because I was far from God, I wasn't protected from danger lurking around the corner. I was stumbling along, looking everywhere for something to fulfill me. The path I had chosen was one of destruction, and I eventually walked right into Satan's snare. It didn't take long before Satan was holding me hostage, bound by the chains of my past. I had been held captive by him before, but I never had a family that would suffer on my behalf. The stakes are much higher when Satan takes a mother captive. My bondage and subsequent captivity could have cost the kingdom thousands of lives for Christ just by rendering me ineffective in my own home. Someone once told me that being a mother was the most important job on earth. I chuckled at the thought of that. How could being a mother be more important than being a disciple or a preacher, a doctor or a missionary? They explained their reasoning to me, and it changed the way I view motherhood. You see, depending on what God has called our children to do, raising our children up in the Lord could affect thousands of lives. Think on that a minute. If Satan can keep you from parenting your children in the knowledge and wisdom of the Lord, he can effectively throw a wrench in the plans God has for your children and their kingdom work. What if you are raising a future disciple, preacher, doctor, or missionary? If Satan can keep them from reaching their potential by poisoning them as a child, that's what he will do. That's exactly what happened to me as a child. Maybe your childhood was also riddled with trauma and abuse. Satan, the father of lies, attacked me from an early age and worked on me until I was a shattered, angry adult, held captive by my flesh. Jesus, in His goodness, came and set me free. He is faithful to do the same for you.

Though my journey seemed long and arduous as I was walking it out, I can look back now and say with certainty that God has always been for me and not against me. I was a broken child who became a broken woman ruled by the flesh. But thankfully, that isn't where my story ended, and it doesn't have to be yours either. If you are willing, God will take you down the road that leads to righteousness.

CHAPTER 2:
Rebellious Roots

The year after my resignation was full of unexpected and difficult emotions. A product of a very messy divorce as a child, I learned early on that when dealing with relationships, jobs, or emotions, the only thing I could bet on was myself. God would reveal to me over the course of the year that if I bet on myself, I would never cash in on the gifts He had waiting for me. All bets are off when you serve Jesus wholeheartedly.

Yes, the year I became a stay-at-home mom was the year God took me to the next level in my relationship with Him. The high I felt from experiencing the goodness of God in my life was incredible. He had fulfilled a prayer that seemed impossible when He sold the farm and produced an income substantial enough to compensate for my salary. He was giving me the desires of my heart and allowing me to stay home with my babies. I never dreamed that I was about to embark on a journey through my lowest valley. The good news is that a valley can only be made when you have a mountain on either side. Glory to God, I had another victory coming, but first, I had to climb.

The first valley I can remember being in resulted in childhood trauma that left a scar. My little sister and I were side by side, experiencing life with our mom as she went through the worst time in her life. My dad was in the military, and we moved around a lot in the short time they were married. We lived in an apartment in Louisville, Kentucky, and when I think of it, I have mostly vague but happy memories. I remember riding my bike with my little sister and playing with neighborhood kids. I can vividly remember trying to pass the swim test to go to the deep end of the community pool. I remember playing Oregon Trail on my giant desktop that sat in my room. There is one memory, though, that is clearer than the rest. In fact, I am able to recall tiny details like what was playing on the TV and what drink my dad had in his hand.

My mom and dad had been arguing a little, leading up to this day. On the last day as a family of four, they were upstairs for a few hours. My mom came down the stairs of our apartment and sat my dad's suitcase at the bottom. She looked at my little sister and me with swollen eyes and a blank look on her face. She half smiled, tears began to flow again, and she turned around and walked back up the stairs, defeated. My little mind began racing and wondering why there was a suitcase at the bottom of the stairs. My dad seemed calm, and so I began asking him questions. He told me over and over again that he was not leaving. I didn't believe him because I made him make a pallet with me on the floor of the living room. I was going to stay up all night with him so that I could be sure he wouldn't leave. The last memory I have of that night was watching "My Three Sons" in black and white on "Nick at Nite." When I woke up, the back door to our apartment was cracked open, and my dad's suitcase was gone. I panicked. I raced upstairs to find my mom, and she told me that he was going to live somewhere else for a while but that he would be back soon. I didn't believe her! I sobbed and I screamed until I fell asleep. I dreamed that he got kidnapped and was in trouble. My tiny mind could not process the fact that the man I called dad would hold me, speak words that he knew were lies and then leave me lying on the floor without a second thought. He didn't even lock the door to protect us from potential danger when he left. I woke up and told my mom that we had to help my dad. She just reassured me that he was okay and that we would be okay, too. I was so angry at her for not caring about where he was! She turned up her soda in a glass bottle, and I, in my rage, hit the bottom of the glass. It landed hard against her lips and rattled her teeth. She silently cried and held me. In the coming weeks, our life would change time and time again, and my emotions were trying to process it all.

Looking back, I cannot imagine how my mother endured what she went through that year. My mom had gotten pregnant with her third child and suffered a miscarriage. My dad, determined to have a boy, came home and told her that he was leaving her for his mistress, who was also pregnant and carrying a boy. She packed his suitcase for him, and that night, he left behind a wife and two daughters in the hope of a new life and a son. The stress from the sudden events my mom experienced caused a disease that had been lying dormant in her body to activate. It activated and attacked her eyes. She went to bed one night and woke up the next morning legally blind. She had lost all vision in her left eye and all central vision in her right. I have often thought of my mother, grieving from the loss of a child, the loss of a husband, and trying to take care of two little girls also experiencing loss. The sheer terror and panic that must have swelled up inside of her the moment she woke up and couldn't see. I don't know how she made it through that week lest God Himself carried her.

We spent the next few days at various doctor appointments trying to figure out what had happened to her sight. When they realized she had suffered irreversible damage, we spent the next few weeks at the Department for the Blind. Newly disabled, she had to learn how to navigate the world around her again, and this took all her time and energy. Our lives were thrown into complete and utter chaos in less than a month. My sister was three, and I was seven at the time. Being the oldest sister meant certain things. It meant I understood the gravity of what was happening a little more than my sister. It meant that I was next in line for the leader of our house when there was a lack of direction. I suddenly became the one to tend to my sister all the time, and this was at no fault of my mom's. It was just the circumstance life had given us. Life had robbed her of her independence, and she fought tooth and nail to learn to adjust and regain it. In the meantime, my sister and I were also learning to navigate the world around us with one less parent and a void that was so dark and bottomless that it seemed like it would never be filled again. Where laughter, smiles, and fun had once filled our days, we were learning to process tears, frustration, unanswered questions, and blank looks on the faces of those we loved. I grew up immediately and learned to take care of my sister through a skewed lens of the world. I had her, and she had me, and as long as we had each other, I would never let anything or anyone take her from me. I became a little mother hen to her and tried my best to shield her from experiencing sadness or pain. I would love her so much that she wouldn't ever have to miss our dad. The trouble with taking care of a child when you are a child yourself is that you forfeit your own childhood in the process. The day my dad left, the little girl I was died, and a controlling people-pleaser was born. I resolved that I would work on myself until no one would want to leave me again. I can remember thinking that if I had been a better daughter and fussed with my sister less, he would have wanted to stay. Maybe if I was more loveable or obedient, he would change his mind and come back. I began to hate myself for making my dad leave. I wanted to take excellent care of my sister and mom so that he might see how good I could be. I wanted to be anything and everything he could ever want in a child so that he wouldn't have to create a new family to have what he wanted.

Of course, now, as an adult, I can clearly see that my dad didn't leave us because I lacked value or worth. But as a child, I lacked the ability to see outside of myself, and I naturally shouldered the blame. By the time I understood the situation for what it was, I was far too old and damaged. The minute he walked out, the devil began filling my tiny mind with untruths. Those untruths echoed in my mind every time I saw a mom, dad, and children together doing anything at all. My soul longed for acceptance and predictability. My character reflected what my soul was desperately seeking to find. I began to knit together a version of me that was sure to unravel the very day someone pulled even the tiniest thread.

When my mom was finished with her therapy at the Department for the Blind, we moved into a one-bedroom apartment with our grandfather in an adult-only complex. His love for us was limitless, and he treated us so kindly. It was a soft place to land and the only place I felt normalcy for a very long time. He was a principal at an elementary school, and he encouraged me to sit down at his Mac computer and write out how I was feeling. Instead of writing down my emotions, I learned to channel my energy into carefully weaving a plot that I could control. I would sit at that bright computer screen and peck away, letter by letter, until I was so lost in the story that I had drowned out the world. He would come out of his bedroom and anxiously read what I had written as if it was the greatest literary piece he had ever had the privilege of reading.

He would tell my teacher how he couldn't wait to see how I would get the character out of the predicament the next day and carry on like I was a genius author waiting for my big break. He gave me hope that my current state wasn't where I would have to stay if I had the ability to write. I found solace in writing because, in a fictional world, if you don't like something, you can erase it and start over. In the real world, that didn't seem to be the case at all.

Fast forward to my first full year as a stay-at-home mom. After the initial excitement wore off, I experienced an identity crisis. I had worked since I was fourteen years old. I enrolled in college at seventeen and earned two degrees. I had three children and was excelling in my career. Teaching left me drained, but that is largely because I was phenomenal at my job. I craved the positive feedback and attention my peers and administrators gave me. I loved being recognized for working hard and helping kids achieve at high levels. I traded in my professional clothes for jeans and tees. I traded the click-clack of high heels (one of my personal favorite things about being a girl) for tennis shoes and flip-flops. My workday consisted of making meals, cleaning messes, going to the grocery store, and tears. I'd like to say the tears were from the tiny people in my house, but the tears were mine. I quickly realized just how much a stay-at-home mom does and how thankless the job is. *Satan didn't want me to enjoy motherhood, and for a while, I let him have his way.*

I cried when I realized I had nowhere to go, no job that needed me. I was hurt that I was replaced in my position by the end of the week. I sobbed the first time I had to swallow my pride and write "unemployed" on paperwork at the pediatrician's office. I felt judged. I felt worthless without an official title or position to hide behind. I felt embarrassed with myself for feeling this way. I didn't realize it then, but I had walked directly into the refiner's fire.

In the following months, I would cry every single day. I remember vividly standing in the shower crying uncontrollably. My husband was sitting in the bathroom, trying his best to make me see what he saw in me.

"Honey, don't you realize how valuable you are to us? We couldn't make it without you."

"You do everything for everyone, and people are always calling you for wisdom and advice. You're irreplaceable."

"You shouldn't be feeling worthless. You are important to so many people, and we could never replace you here."

It didn't matter what my sweet husband said, though. My heart was determined to believe that I was useless. That I had no worth or value. Day after day, I let Satan feed me these lies. Looking back, I imagine Satan himself pushing me down and kicking me repeatedly until I was curled up in the fetal position, begging for it to stop. At the time, I couldn't see it for what it was. My feelings defied logic, reason, and biblical wisdom. I spiraled into a depression and began to have dark thoughts. I never felt like I wanted to kill myself, but I began fixating on what my husband's life would be like without me around. The devil would whisper, "He would be so much more peaceful without you crying and being dramatic all the time." "He'd have so much more money if he wasn't having to support you." "Maybe he could sit down and rest without having to deal with all your emotional baggage." "He will find a wife that will be a cook and housewife. He deserves that." I internalized all of these lies until I began to extend those thoughts onto my children. The devil started, "Your kids are going to need therapy from dealing with a sad mom." "You are emotionally damaging them when you get mad and yell at them." "They are only going to remember how sad and angry their mom was all the time." In turn, I would lay in my bed or stand in the shower and cry silent tears that couldn't be stopped. The sorrow I felt within my soul would take my breath and leave me unable to do anything but the bare minimum.

I became a robot, able to display different emotions on demand. I didn't want my kids to know I was sad, so I became a master pretender. I could turn off my emotions and portray whatever version of me everyone needed at the time. I went through motions of cleaning, cooking, tending to the needs of others, and for a while, maybe I even fooled myself. I rarely displayed any emotion but happiness. I compartmentalized any negative emotions, putting them off for another day. That day came one afternoon and was quite unexpected. For no reason at all, I exploded on my husband. I was in my car driving and talking to him on the phone. We began to argue, and the emotions I had been ignoring so well came barreling to the surface at lightning speed. I reached an intersection and briefly looked both ways, then pulled out. Before I could internalize what had happened, my car was spinning out of control. I had been hit from the side, and I never saw it coming. The phone flew out of my hand, the airbags deployed, and before I could so much as scream, the car abruptly came to a stop. As I sat there, tears began to flow. I was terrified at what had happened and thankful that I was alive, largely unhurt. I was overcome with emotion because while my car was spinning, all I could think of was my babies and my husband. More than that, the name of Jesus almost audibly filled my car. Jesus, Jesus, Jesus. It is hard to articulate in words, but it felt like the air around me was crying out to the Son of God. His presence filled my car. It was a life-altering moment for me and my walk with the Lord.

My husband was terrified because he heard the wreck and then the deafening, albeit brief, silence that followed. I was unable to reach my phone, and the wreck left me breathless for a few moments. By the time my husband arrived on scene, I was a complete mess of emotions. I was sobbing uncontrollably and hugging the strangers that had hit me. I was so thankful that they were not hurt because of my carelessness. When my husband took me home, he held me while I cried. I cried and confessed how I had been feeling. That I was struggling with thoughts of "what-if." I didn't want to die, but I also didn't feel like I wanted to live. God used that wreck, that all-consuming fire of God moment in my car, to jolt me back into reality. *I did want to live. A lot.* As we lay in bed and my husband heard how

I had been feeling, he began to speak life over me. He began to remind me who God says I am. He had done this dozens of times before, except this time, because of my experience with Jesus, my heart was ready to receive it. Do you hear what I am telling you? Satan will almost take us out if we give him just an inch of space in our mind. I hadn't only given him an inch; I had surrendered my entire head space to him and his lies. I let him hold me hostage, a prisoner in my own mind. Looking back, I have no idea why I didn't act immediately when I began having self-destructive thoughts. I don't know if I wasn't as familiar with the Word of God as I am now and didn't know what to do or if I was already too battle-weary to put up a fight. Regardless, my inability to act was a definite sign of the lukewarm water I had been marinating in for a very long time. And God doesn't do lukewarm. At all. Thankfully, He loves us enough to heat things up a bit and put us in the middle of a fire.

I'd like to tell myself that this was the first time I had felt like I just didn't care about myself, but in the spirit of transparency, that isn't true. At the root of most of my problems was a lack of self-worth. I got drunk for the first time when I was fourteen. I was at my dad's house with my dad, uncles, and cousins. My cousins and I had been sneaking alcohol out of the kitchen, and before long, I found myself standing at the counter trying to pour a Pepsi with the lid still on the two-liter. My dad was in the kitchen with me when this happened, and he was staring at me with a puzzled look on his face. For a moment, I froze in fear, thinking I might be in trouble. Instead, my dad belly laughed and called all my uncles into the room to tell them I was drunk. From that day forward, I believed that I wasn't even valuable enough to keep sober. Thankfully, I never experimented with drugs, but that was only because partying and drinking were fun enough for me. When I drank alcohol, everything seemed like it didn't matter. I lived for the moment with no regard for the future at all. I felt happier, if only for a few minutes. With enough alcohol, I could be the life of the party, and for a people-pleaser, that meant the world. In addition to that, I gained a group of friends that I partied with all the time. Alcohol gave us memories that were funny to talk about the next day, and we did things that gave us a common bond. I finally felt like I belonged. I had "people," and they wanted me around.

I got married to a boy from my hometown, and for a while, we continued on the same path of destruction. We were stationed in Fort Benning, Georgia, and let me just tell you, nobody parties harder than the army. When I got pregnant with our first child, though, something in my heart shifted. Months earlier, I had met a woman that would eventually become my best friend. She and her husband were youth pastors, and she happened to teach kindergarten in the room right next to mine. She had invited me to church, but I didn't go at first. I was raised in and around church, but we only went sporadically at best. I just didn't have a desire to give up what I was doing and go to church. Nevertheless, she would gently tell me how much Jesus loved me, and she never judged me. I could show up hungover from the night before, and she would smile the most genuine smile and was happy to see me just the same. Her behavior intrigued me so much. Though we had virtually nothing in common, we had a strong bond and real friendship, and so her influence on me naturally grew. I finally accepted her invitation to church when I was six or so months pregnant. I don't remember what the sermon was, but I remember weeping the entire time. I didn't want to be the me I was before. I didn't want this precious boy growing in my belly to know anything but love and acceptance. I wanted him to have a mom and a dad, together and healthy, all the days of his life. God was beginning to awaken a part of me that had been there since before I was born. I was feeling the void that only Jesus can fill, and He was gently softening my heart in preparation for His invitation there.

The roots of my sin began when I was just a little girl. Even at the young age of seven, the devil was fighting for my soul. He poisoned my mind and made me believe I wasn't worthy of love. Once roots are firmly planted, they provide life, or death, to the whole tree. My roots continued to poison me for years. My lack of self-worth would plague my marriage, taint my ability to parent my children well, and create drama when I overstepped boundaries trying to control everyone around me. God knew if He didn't get to the root of the problem with me, I wouldn't experience life the way he intended me to.

Poisonous roots not only kill the body, they crush the soul in the process. Even worse than death is the dying process. It's the destructive thought patterns and lack of self-worth that keep you up at night, staring up at the ceiling, wondering why you can't just be okay. It's painful and slow, and the cycle feels like it is never-ending. Do you believe that God is able to take your hurt, your twisted ways of thinking, and your trauma and give you new life? I am living proof that He can and will. **"Jesus answered, 'I am the way and the truth and the life. No one comes to the Father except through me'"** (John 14:6).

For the remainder of this book, I am going to assume you have accepted Jesus into your heart and know Him. If you haven't yet, I encourage you to take the leap and do it now. Wherever you are is the perfect place to do it. It's as simple as saying, "God, I know You created me and love me more than I can imagine. I want You to live in my heart and save my soul. I believe that You sent Your Son, Jesus, to die on the cross for my sins, and I believe that He rose again on the third day, conquering death and the grave. I will tell of Your goodness all the days of my life."

Now that you know the circumstances that broke me, let's talk about how He put me back together and made me beautiful again. More importantly, let's find out what it takes to live a victorious, joyful life so you can experience your life the way God intended it!

CHAPTER 3:
Beauty for Ashes

By now, you have probably relived some of your own trauma as you have read a glimpse into mine. Maybe yours was much more damaging and the torment more severe. Perhaps it wasn't as traumatic as mine. No matter where you fall on the spectrum, unless you are sanctified and redeemed by the blood of Jesus, you have something that keeps you up at night and torments you relentlessly because that is what the devil does. The devil placed a target on your back a long time ago. He has been pursuing you ever since. He wants you to have zero satisfaction in life, so you are always searching for the next thing. He wants your victories to be far and few between so that you stay frustrated and defeated. He wants you to find comfort in the bottom of a glass of wine, a couple of nerve pills, or sexual pleasures outside of marriage. He wants nothing more than for you to stay wounded and unhealed so that you remain bitter and full of hatred. He wants your soul. And he will do anything to get it. He will even go so far as to trick you and make you think that you are doing what the Lord wants you to do. He will have you believing that the twenty-five-year-old down the street with her new-age feminism is preaching the gospel when she tells you her interpretation of the Word. He won't make you question the youth pastor with his man bun and skinny jeans telling you everything is all good if you feel good and love others. He will have you spend your time on TikTok and YouTube listening to clips of preachers interpreting the Word. If you aren't careful, he will have your brain twisted in confusion. He will have you purposely listening to false teachers and preachers before you have had a chance to read it for yourself. You'll wind up worse off than when you started, and you won't even think you are doing anything wrong.

We have opinions on every corner, promising victory and joy, but end up disappointed and discouraged when we don't feel a change in our lives. Unless we pick up our Bibles and spend time in the living Word of God, we will never experience all He has for us in this life. Why do we never just go straight to the source? We can't heal, we can't have victory and joy if we don't know what God requires of us to get there. You wouldn't leave New York to go to California by piecing together several directions that different people told you, blindly leaving your fate up to them. You would open up an atlas or an app and plan your route according to the roadmap. So why do so many of us let the devil trick us into trusting our eternal destiny to everyone but the source? We live in a generation that will listen to anyone and everyone instead of going to the one who created us and knows us more intimately than we know ourselves. I mean, if the goal is to get to heaven, why would you trust anyone but the Lord to get you there? One thing I know for sure is that if you want to find true joy in Jesus, you have a relationship with Him.

On our quest from ruins to redemption, we are going to have to drown out the noise. Turn off the TV, give social media a rest. Redemption will be found only by building an intimate relationship with God. As you begin to build your relationship, it's important to remember what it takes to make a real relationship work effectively. It requires commitment, effort, and always showing up. It requires that you do your part.

Marriage, for example, isn't operating at its best when one spouse takes on assignments or responsibilities that are not designed for them or if they neglect the things they are responsible for. These things can be emotional needs, physical needs, or even obligations that take your time and energy. If either spouse isn't fulfilling their roles effectively, the marriage bond is fractured. Over time, the fracture will lead to a complete separation. Often, one party is shocked that the marriage is suddenly in dire need of attention because they have fallen into the hypnotic rhythm of the familiar. Familiarity breeds content, and sometimes, we can become content with unhealthy habits and relationships.

The same thing can happen in our relationship with God. We know we are saved and love God. We go to church on Sunday morning. We bless our food before we eat. We pray for others, and we try to live honest, kind lives. In short, we check all the "Christian" boxes. What we may not realize is that while we are comfortable checking all the boxes, we also become stagnant. We might look good on paper, but a closer look would show that we are just going through the motions. It's in this comfort zone that Satan loves to sneak in and steal joy and replace it with defeat. This is exactly where I was when I began my journey with Jesus as a stay-at-home mom. Jesus didn't hang on the cross for us to be defeated, joyless "box-checking Christians"! He died on the cross and defeated death and the grave so we could boldly operate our gifts and authority here on this earth! We have the power and authority to move mountains, bind demons, and boldly pray if only we recognize that authority!

God can take the most hopeless situation and fix it beyond our wildest dreams. He can take the dream you have buried in your heart and make it come to fruition. He can repair your marriage, heal your sickness, cure your broken heart. He can move mountains and appoint and remove kings as He pleases. There is nothing our God can't do. I'm sure you agree with me. I'm sure most believers would. The problem is that most women I know don't walk in the authority of this absolute truth. If we believe that God can do anything, why do so many of God's children swim in lukewarm waters, drowning in depression, smothering in anxiety, praying weak, ineffective prayers?

I'm serious. I know so many people whose prayers sound more like a sad anthem of their lives than a powerful petition taken to the King. Their words almost drip with unbelief. What happens when we put words like that out into the atmosphere? Do the heavenly hosts rejoice and sing? Do demons quiver and hide? It isn't God's will for our lives that we are sick, discouraged, and downtrodden all the time! He wants to give us beauty for ashes! God wants to fellowship with us so that He can heal our wounds from the inside out. But fellowship requires relationship. What are you doing to work on your relationship with your Creator? We must put ourselves in a position to know, understand, and apply the Word of God in our lives so intentionally and effectively that nothing can fracture our relationship with God.

Just like women come in all shapes and sizes, we come in all spiritual shapes and sizes, too. Some of us have been walking with the Lord for a long time. Some of us might be new here. Some of us might be on the other side of the fence looking over to see if we'd like to open the gate. If we were sitting in my living room drinking coffee and hanging out, we could talk about where we are in our journey to the cross for the next several hours. But since you are there and I am here, let's just agree that we all carry baggage that needs to be unpacked. Some of our suitcases are lighter than others, but we can't carry any of them ourselves as we travel on the road toward heaven. What truly matters is how we unpack our baggage and allow God to do the heavy lifting. Even after we lay it down and let God carry it, we must find out why we insisted on carrying it for so long in the first place. This is the part in our journey as women that we try so hard to avoid.

It's not the carrying that feels hard. We carry the mental load of our families every single day and make it look effortless. We carry our children in our bellies for nine months at a time and come out on the other side with a beautiful human. We carry our friendships with the utmost care and concern. We have zero problem with carrying our baggage. But if you ask us to unpack it, yikes. That's going to take some time. When you have been on a trip, you bring all kinds of things back that you didn't plan on. Tags and receipts thrown into the suitcase. Maybe some new items that you really didn't need. Perhaps a seashell or sand that made you happy and content while you were on your trip but now aggravate you and make you angry sitting in the bottom crevices of your suitcase. Once you separate it, you have to organize it. You will wash the clothes, throw away the trash, and put away new items. You will have to put away the freshly washed clothes. All of this takes so much time and energy. It throws you right back into the routine and work that you needed a vacation from in the first place. I don't know about you, but I always dread the unpacking. It just takes so much more time than carrying it around in the trunk or shutting it up in the closet. Our emotional baggage is the same. This is the suitcase we put our unpleasant emotions and experiences in. Some old memories that have faded with time, fresh wounds that are still healing, every hurt and disappointment. The trauma we don't talk about. It's all in there. We don't want to take the time to deal with what's inside, but we also don't want to sit it down. We want to keep it close by us so no one else picks it up and sees the garbage we have been carrying with us.

I carried my baggage everywhere I went my entire childhood and most of my adult life. When I decided to move closer to Jesus and trust Him more, God insisted that we pop the latch on my baggage. The trouble in that was that the mess I'd been carrying around, tucked away for no one to see, came spilling out. When God got ready to help me clean it up, I had to identify what was inside and why I kept it there so long. This process was hard and painful, but God was faithful in showing me what I needed to do to live in victory and authority.

God gives us all the answers we will ever need tucked right in the pages of His Word. He is the master potter. He can take a broken vessel and turn it into the most beautiful, unique, and useful piece you've ever seen. His Word tells us that He will literally take our ashes and give us a crown of beauty, the oil of joy, instead of mourning (Isaiah 61:3). This is what God did for me, and the tradeoff began the day I decided I wanted a meaningful relationship with Him; the day I let Him open my baggage and help me sort it out.

This is what God will do for you, too. He is ready to pour the oil of gladness over you, but how do you get in position to feel the first drop? It's so much easier than people think. God wants you to be full of the joy of the Lord, and He wants to heal your broken heart so you can go into the world and tell others of His goodness and grace!

> » The first step to victory is inviting Jesus into your heart to live. If you've already done this, great! If not, I encourage you to do it now. He is ready and waiting on you!

> » Once He's inside your heart, you must be filled with His truth!! His Word, the sword of the Spirit, is your weapon against the enemy! When you have the belt of truth fitted firmly around your waist, ready to yield the sword of the Spirit at a moment's notice, the devil knows he has met his match!

» As you learn His Word, you must begin to apply it to your everyday life. God wants a relationship with you! God is faithful to do what He says. You also must be willing to live out His Word and commands.

» Talk to Him every single day. Do you know His voice? Listen to Him when He speaks. It's often subtle and small but persistent, nonetheless. God often speaks to me while I am doing the most ordinary things. My house is quiet during the day, and as I clean and run errands, I listen to worship music and talk to the Lord, sometimes audibly and sometimes in my head. I have learned over time that He will drop an idea or a person in my spirit, and as I pray about my thoughts, He leads me into what He wants to reveal to me. Hearing from God doesn't have to be this monumental moment where the ground shakes and you hear a voice. For me, it's always been a gentle whisper that grows louder as I think on it.

» When you hear Him direct you to do something, you have to be ready and willing to obey! Not sure if God is speaking to you? Try the simple test I use to determine whose voice you are hearing. I ask myself, "Would the devil be happy if I _____?" Followed by, "Would God get the glory if I did _____?" For example, if I think I am supposed to give money to someone, I ask myself, "Would the devil be pleased with me for giving money to this single mother? Would God get the glory if I do it humbly and follow His rules for giving?" Depending on how I answer those two questions, I commit the act to the Lord and do it as I feel He is leading me, or I pray on it and ask God to clearly show me if it is from Him. Obviously, this is only the method I use if I feel like God is asking me to do something, and it isn't foolproof. You have to seek the Lord and ask Him to guide you and give you wisdom. He is faithful to do it. I have found that the less likely I am to do something in my normal routine, the more often it is the Lord nudging me to do it. The Lord often requires me to do things that are outside of my comfort zone. He wants me to trust and obey. It's easy to do the things I normally do, but when God asks me to do something that I can't predict the outcome of, I get to decide if I am going to fully trust Him or not. It's in this place that I level up or down in my walk with Him. There is no standing still when it comes to God. I'll give you an example from my own life. I will be in a hurry in a store, and as I am checking out, the Lord will abruptly plant the idea in my mind that I should ask the cashier if there is anything I can pray for them about. I never, and I mean never, want to do this. I almost always wrestle with God a minute. But every single time I have done it, the cashiers have either been brought to tears or will tell me something that they are dealing with that is heavy. We plant good seeds on foreign soil when we are obedient to Christ.

» Finally, you must allow God to take the wounds of your past and heal them completely. This requires intimate trust and sometimes painful obedience. It isn't easy to take wounds we want to keep hidden and willingly expose them to God. The devil wants us to be so protective of our wounds that carrying them around feels like a badge of honor. Don't fall for his schemes. You have to allow God to transform you from the inside out. Your ability to give God your trauma and pain and heal you is a critical step to attaining victory, walking in righteousness, and experiencing joy!

If we commit to practicing these few things every day without tiring out or giving up, God is faithful to transform us from the inside out. The church of old was an all-consuming fire that changed the atmosphere when they started to fan the flames. Do you believe that God's goodness is within your reach? Are you sold out on the idea that God can really trade beauty for ashes?

CHAPTER 4:
Zion

> "The Spirit of the Sovereign Lord is on me, because the Lord has anointed me to proclaim good news to the poor. He has sent me to bind up the brokenhearted, to proclaim freedom for the captives and release from darkness for the prisoners, to proclaim the year of the Lord's favor and the day of vengeance of our God, to comfort all who mourn, and provide for those who grieve in Zion—to bestow on them a crown of beauty instead of ashes, the oil of joy instead of mourning and a garment of praise instead of a spirit of despair. They will be called oaks of righteousness, a planting of the Lord for the display of his splendor."
>
> ISAIAH 61:1–3

God outlines hope for even the most desperately broken soul in three tiny verses. Look at the words that He uses to describe who He is sending help to: the poor, the brokenhearted, the captives, the prisoners sitting in darkness, those who have been done wrong, the ones who mourn, the ones who grieve, those who are stuck in a pit of despair. Surely, the hurt you have buried in your heart can be found tucked in the message of Isaiah 61:1–3. While He highlights the hurt of mankind, what He offers to trade for it feels to good to be true! His offer is for good news, freedom, the light in the darkness, vengeance, comfort, relief, joy, and praise!

The only requirement is that you must be in the right place at the right time. Zion. And since Zion is a literal place in Jerusalem, is this scripture even referring to any of us today? *Yes*! Zion is known to be both a physical place and a spiritual dwelling in the Bible. "Zion" can be anywhere God dwells. In your bathroom floor where you are curled up in a ball, weeping silently so no one hears your anguish. In the car while you are driving around in circles, trying to figure it all out. In the doctor's office, when they share news that grips your heart with fear. Zion is a place we can get to today, and since it is the dwelling place of God, I desperately want to live there. It is in Zion that God will take the ashes of your past and give you the glorious splendor fit for a queen.

How can you be sure that you have made your heart a dwelling place for God? I think the answer is surprisingly simple. Be like David and just ask Him. In Psalm 14:5, David tells us that **"God is present in the company of the righteous."** In other words, He dwells with those whose lives are righteous. God, because He confirms and never contradicts Himself, graciously reassures us that living righteously is the way to dwell with Him again in Isaiah 61. He tells us that when we are in Zion making our trade, we will be called "oaks of righteousness." Coincidence? Absolutely not.

The biblical definition of righteousness is to act in accord with divine or moral law: to be free from guilt or sin. The word itself seems so intimidating. In searching for righteousness, I have compared myself to other women—women I feel are holier than me—whatever that means. In the past, I have used the scale of comparison to evaluate my righteousness. You might be guilty of this, too. My internal dialogue would sound something like this:

"I know she reads her Bible more than me because she posts her open Bible and coffee pic every day on social media. Why don't I get up and do that?"

"She brings a notebook and takes notes when the pastor is talking, and she even uses different color ink to represent different things. Why don't I have that level of commitment and organization?"

"She speaks with authority and knows Scripture inside and out. Her prayers are always so powerful. Why can't I be more like her??

"She never loses her temper with her kids but always seems to make the right choice at the right time, showing grace and mercy instead of anger and a short fuse. Why can't I be a mother like she is?"

I could rattle off these thoughts all day because I have a lifetime's worth of material to pull from. Comparison is a thief of joy and will rob you of your rightful place in Zion if you let it.

I stayed stuck in this cycle for years. The danger in this cycle is that the longer I allowed myself to entertain pervasive thoughts, the worse off my mental state would become. Discouragement would settle in, and I would lose motivation to strive for righteousness. I have an all-or-nothing personality, and sometimes that leaves me longing for what I decide "perfection" looks like. If I feel like I am not measuring up to that level of perfection, I throw in the towel and don't try at all. I hate to do anything half-heartedly. When comparing myself to other sisters in Christ, I painted a picture of perfection. The trouble was it wasn't anything like who I am naturally. I am not organized enough to carry pens of every color and a notebook to every service. And on the off chance that I did put a bunch of pens in my purse, my children would get them out of there and write all over the pages of the notebook before I even remembered them. I don't read my Bible at the crack of dawn every morning because I need a full hour of drinking coffee and letting my failing eyesight wake up so that I can focus. I am just not a morning person. At all. Early morning Bible reading, with comprehension, just doesn't work for me. I get overstimulated after wearing so many hats all day and sometimes don't have Mary Poppins patience with my children. I'm not everyone's cup of tea. In fact, my circle is small. I study the Word of God, and I don't back down when an unbiblical situation arises. I will be the first person to point out Scripture and tell someone their thoughts are not aligned with biblical standards of living. This has become increasingly dividing in the politically charged era we are living in today. So yeah, everyone doesn't just light up when I walk in the room. I say all of that to explain that we will never be able to truly attain righteousness if we are trying to walk to Zion in someone else's shoes. Put on your own shoes, lace them up, and get to walking. God created you with a specific purpose in mind.

I once read a motivational poster somewhere that said something like this:

"God looked down on all the earth and the people in it. He thought, *This is good, but you know what would make it even better?* And then He created *you.*"

He loves you just as you are because you are His magnificent creation. Psalm 139:13–16 tells us exactly what happened the moment you were created.

> "For you created my inmost being; you knit me together in my mother's womb. I praise you because I am fearfully and wonderfully made; your works are wonderful, I know that full well. My frame was not hidden from you when I was made in the secret place, when I was woven together in the depths of the earth. Your eyes saw my unformed body; all the days ordained for me were written in your book before one of them came to be."

Righteousness is attainable for you. And me. God will allow us to enter Zion even though we don't have it all together, judging by the world's standards. Or even our own crazy, unattainable standards. He doesn't even care if we get up before the roosters to study and read. He simply cares that we do it. Fancy pens with lots of organization don't impress Him in the least. His standards of righteousness are different than ours.

If we can't work harder, read more, or be more organized to become righteous, just what does God expect us to do? Luckily for us, we have the Bible to guide us and answer all the questions that we have. David didn't have the luxury of the written Word of God, so he had to go straight to the source (which is also available to us today). Let's look at the conversation David had with God as recorded in Psalm 15:1–5: **"Lord, who may dwell in your sacred tent? Who may live on your holy mountain?"**

David asks God an honest question here. He wants to know who can dwell, or live, with God. God is faithful to answer him.

> "The one whose walk is blameless, who does what is righteous, who speaks the truth from their heart (this is God's truth tucked away in the heart of the believer); who tongue utters no slander, who does no wrong to his neighbor, and casts no slur on others; who despises a vile person but honors those who fear the Lord; who keeps an oath even when it hurts and does not change their mind, who lends money to the poor with no interest; who does not accept a bribe against the innocent. Whoever does these things will not be shaken."

Wow. David asked, and God clearly laid out the answer. God is clear and precise in His language and instruction. He illustrates for us an "if this, then this" scenario throughout Scripture. The answer to who can dwell in Zion and the reward for righteousness are prime examples of this.

God is saying that *if* you want to dwell with Him, *then* you have to be blameless, righteous, speak His truth, don't talk bad about or tell lies about others, make decisions that are reflective of a life lived for Him, hate what God calls sin, freely give, and live with integrity. If you feel God is distant, check yourself against these standards and work to fix what you are lacking. In this way, you will draw close to God. If you don't know where to start, that's okay too. If you'll take the first step, God is faithful to meet you on the next.

The people of Zion must meet a higher standard than anywhere else, but that's because the reward of living there is more peaceful and joyful than anywhere else. And the best part is that you get to live with God!

God created the universe and everything in it with such precision and order that I am led to believe that nothing is happenstance with Him. When God speaks, the order of His words is precisely chosen and has purpose. In the verses we just examined, he mentions being blameless and then righteous, in that order. These characteristics are cut from the same heavenly cloth, so let's look at them under a microscope. Except I don't really have a microscope, and you can't put words in a petri dish, but I digress. Let's just agree to take a closer look.

When I was a sixth-grade teacher, we studied bartering and trading. Each year, at the end of the unit, we would have a "Barter and Trade" day. The parents and guardians would sign permission slips acknowledging that their child could both bring items to school and then also trade said items. The kids looked forward to this day each year and began planning for it at the beginning of the unit. They understood that what they needed to bring had to have a high value and be something other kids would want. If they brought items nobody wanted, no kid in their right mind would trade something of value for it. On the day of the event, the kids would set their desks up with their items for trade placed carefully on top. Kids in other classrooms did the same thing. And then, finally, we would release one classroom at a time to walk around and try to barter and trade. I loved to listen to the conversations between kids when they found something that was particularly valuable to them. They would plead their case so carefully and try to convince the other student to complete the transaction. Sometimes, it would work, and sometimes, they would leave with the same item in tow. The lesson the kids learned was that, as people, we only trade things of equal or similar value.

I don't know if you realize this or not, but obtaining righteousness is a trade you make, too. It's hard to believe, but on the day that you accept Jesus into your heart and decide to give your life to Him, in exchange for your sin, He gives you righteousness. Yes, He takes something worthless and gives you the most precious, invaluable gift you will ever receive. It's a mystery to me how God could love us enough to send His Son to die an excruciating death in exchange for the shame, guilt, and evil intentions of a sinful people who might not even appreciate it for the miracle that it is. But that is why I am me and not God. His love for us is unexplainable and hard to comprehend.

When Christ died on the cross, He took on the sin of all mankind. Second Corinthians 5:21 tells us: **"God made him who had no sin (Jesus) to be sin for us, so that in him we might become the righteousness of God."**

He became sin and made atonement for you and me at the crucifixion.

CHAPTER 5:
This Mystery Is History! No, Really, It's History

To understand the complexity of the exchange, I think it's important to stop and learn a little bit of biblical history. Before Jesus died on the cross and became our sacrificial lamb, God required a blood sacrifice, or atonement, for the sins of the people. Most people who have studied the Bible at all know and understand this. But there is a complexity to it that is fascinating and helps understand the importance of each rule and law that God had prior to the death of Jesus. God had rules for how everyone should atone for their sins, including the common person (see Leviticus 4:27), the priests (see Leviticus 4:3), the leaders (Leviticus 4:22) and the nation (Leviticus 4:13). Atonement, at its most basic explanation, is reparation for wrongdoing. Each of these different groups of people had different requirements for how and what they should sacrifice for atonement, but they all had to shed blameless blood in order for reparations to be made.

CHAPTER 5: THIS MYSTERY IS HISTORY! NO, REALLY, IT'S HISTORY

In Leviticus 17:11, God tells the Israelites, **"For the life of a creature is in the blood, and I have given it to you to make atonement for yourselves on the altar; it is the blood that makes atonement for one's life."**

The longer I study the Word of God, the more aware I become of who God really is. I know God is perfect and without flaw, but seeing how He delicately and specifically weaves the details of the Bible together creates a beautiful description of the word "perfectionist." He leaves nothing to happenstance, and no detail is without intention. He clearly demonstrates His attention to detail when we see how He foreshadows events that will happen much later on in Scripture.

Atonement is one of the most beautiful examples of how God foreshadows what is to come. When God is authoring the story, the events always come full circle. When God met Moses on Mount Sinai, He gave him the Ten Commandments, and He also gave him instructions for building the Tabernacle. The Tabernacle would consist of an outer court, a room called the Holy Place, and another room behind the Holy Place called the Most Holy Place. In between the Holy Place and the Most Holy Place was a curtain separating the two rooms. Both of these places were set apart for God so that the priests could sacrifice and worship Him there. The priests entered the Holy Place daily to pray and worship God and burn incense at the altar of incense, but the Most Holy Place could only be entered once a year on the Day of Atonement.

You can read about the Day of Atonement in depth in Leviticus, chapter 16, in the Old Testament. Until then, I will try my best to summarize it for you here. The Day of Atonement was the holiest, most significant day of the year for Israelites. Since Jesus had not yet been crucified on the cross, the Israelites could not simply ask God for forgiveness as we can today. A blood exchange was required. So, they were instructed by God to make atonement for their sin through a blood sacrifice. This was done by the sacrificing of choice animals, free of blemish or defect, as directed by God. The people confessed their sins, and the high priest went into the Most Holy Place to make atonement for them as a nation.

The Most Holy Place also housed the Ark of the Covenant and the atonement cover (also called God's mercy seat).

> "The Lord said to Moses: 'Tell your brother Aaron that he is not to come whenever he chooses into the Most Holy place behind the curtain in front of the atonement cover of the ark, or else he will die. For I will appear in a cloud over the atonement cover on the ark.'"
>
> LEVITICUS 16:2

The Most Holy Place was the dwelling place of God Himself, and because sin still separated people from God, they could not go in and out of His presence freely. The curtain separating the Holy from the Most Holy symbolized our inaccessibility to God prior to Jesus. Atonement only covered sin so that it was forgiven. The blood of Jesus *removed* sin when He died on the cross. Sometimes, one word can make all the difference. Covering of sin would work for a time, but the removal of sin was the better way.

Jesus became sin for all of humanity when He died on the cross. A life for a life. (It's okay to cry at the part. It always makes me cry, too.) When His blood poured out of Him on the cross and He suffered a death more excruciating than He deserved, He atoned our sins and removed the barrier that existed between God and people.

> "And when Jesus had cried out again in a loud voice, he gave up his spirit. At that moment the curtain of the temple was torn in two from top to bottom. The earth shook, the rocks split and the tombs broke open."
>
> MATTHEW 27:50–51

When the curtain was literally torn in two at the moment Jesus gave up His spirit, it was figuratively torn as well. God was symbolically showing all of humanity that the barrier between Him and us had been removed. At that moment, God became freely accessible, and our sin became eligible for complete removal. In other words, *we can finally be found blameless in His sight.*

mic drop

And with that revelation, we have come full circle. We are made blameless and righteous on the day we exchange our sins for His truth! How awesome is that?

The way to become morally blameless and righteous by God's standards simply requires that you accept Jesus as your personal Savior and ask forgiveness for your sins. As we just learned, Jesus made us blameless when He died on the cross. Will we stay blameless after we get saved? Well, Lord no. We are humans, after all. We will continually falter and sin because we are constantly fighting the flesh. The way that we stay blameless and righteous is to live a life that mirrors the Word of God.

We will spend a lifetime asking God over and over again to make us blameless in His sight by repenting and asking God to forgive us. Repentant hearts are hearts that are truly sorry for the sin. I hear more people than I care to admit decide to do something they know is sinful because they will just ask God to forgive them when "it" (the sin they are committing) is over. They make a plan to reap the benefit of the flesh and be forgiven in the spirit. It doesn't work that way. This is an abuse of the mercy and grace of God. Perverting the Word of God and using His grace and mercy carelessly is a dangerous game to play. I'm not implying that, as humans, we will never slip up and do something we know we shouldn't. I am talking about the repeated and careless sins that we partake in because we know God is a forgiving God. One of the fruits of the Spirit is self-control. A woman on her way to Zion demonstrates self-control more times than not, and when she does stumble in her walk, she is quick to ask forgiveness from a heart that is grieved by her sin.

Are you more concerned with satisfying the flesh, or are you more concerned with presenting a blameless life to the Lord? Righteousness begins with being more concerned with how God views you and your behavior than anything else. When your heart is turned toward God, the Holy Spirit will naturally make your heart tender to the commands of God and your relationship with Him.

Attaining righteousness and blamelessness sounds so simple. And in a lot of ways, it is. But things are not always as easy as they seem for some of us. I did not truly dwell with God and understand His nature fully for a long time after I got saved. I could not be totally righteous and blameless before Him until I faced my hidden sins head-on. Come on, sis, don't give me that look. You know full well what sin I am talking about. These are the sins that you keep close by you. To be fair, you might not even realize that they are sins. Maybe they are stuffed in with some of your baggage that you carry around from living in brokenness for so long. Maybe they have been tucked away so discreetly that you don't even realize the sinful patterns you are stuck in. This was the case for me. I had a hidden sin tucked so perfectly inside my childhood baggage that I failed to see it at all until the Holy Spirit graciously revealed it to me.

I can say with certainty that after I got saved, I still struggled with sadness and depression quite a bit. I think there are lots of women who would say they felt that way, too. Maybe you are even struggling with this now. I couldn't understand why it was harder for me to experience joy after I got saved than it was before. I had given up the alcohol. I gave up cussing and living like *hell*. I quit going out and partying until I puked. I was reading my Bible, faithfully attending church, and pressing into Jesus. But I was also repeatedly allowing sin to control my life. The control it had over me was so pervasive and powerful that it kept me from experiencing victory.

CHAPTER 6:
The Golden Calf

Growing up in the '80s meant certain things. It meant that somewhere in your mama's kitchen décor was a duck with an apron on, and somewhere in your house, the Ten Commandments were displayed. You probably also had that brown sofa (you know the one I am talking about) and some wood paneling in your house that those Ten Commandments hung on. Even though we moved around a lot, my mama always hung up an 11x17 picture of the Ten Commandments. Oftentimes, I would fixate on the old familiar picture and obsessively try to memorize what it said (control freak, remember?). I would read those commandments over and over, cementing the words in my mind. Then, as a test to myself, I would close my eyes and try to recite them as fast as I could. The words were written on my heart long before I was old enough to understand them. As I grew in my understanding of the Lord, I still didn't fully realize the entirety of all the commandments in my own life and my disobedience of them until one random afternoon driving home after work.

Let's look at them again in case you need a refresher.

1. You shall have no other gods before me.
2. You shall not have false idols.
3. Do not take the name of the Lord your God in vain.
4. Remember the Sabbath day to keep it holy.
5. Honor your father and your mother.
6. You shall not murder.
7. You shall not commit adultery.
8. You shall not steal.
9. You shall not bear false witness against your neighbor.
10. You shall not covet.

Remember that the biblical definition of righteousness is to "act in accordance with divine or moral law." It is clear that God is setting a moral standard for His people with the Ten Commandments. Some of the commandments have been written into law in our country. You can't steal or murder someone and get away with it. Others have been woven into our societal code of ethics. The majority of them are easy enough not to do for most of the population. Lying, cheating, stealing, jealous, cursing, disrespectful people don't really make for good humans. The rest of the commandments feel so blatantly obvious that God's people would be appalled at even an accusation of engaging in that kind of sin. I mean, what kind of Christian has false idols or other gods? Surely not the real deal, sanctified ones! *Gasp.* Except what if we do? The Holy Spirit gently began nudging me years ago and revealed to me how I worshipped false idols every single day. Not only did I worship false idols, I let my worship become so out of control that it hindered my family, my friends, and even my witness.

If you are going to allow God to heal you, you have to be okay with Him going below the surface of the wound. He goes all the way to our roots. No matter how old they are or how deep they go, God needs to show you the root of your pain so He can completely heal your heart. Revealing the root of unrighteousness and, therefore, your sin is a necessary step to gaining freedom and walking victoriously in Christ.

God uses symbolism and nature throughout the Bible. He

created both, and so it only makes sense that they mirror each other. God intricately designed every piece of the universe, and I like to think that He gave us nature to better understand ourselves and our relationship with Him. In nature, the roots of a tree will die for three main reasons. If the tree has poor drainage and becomes oversaturated with water, it will eventually drown. If the tree is covered in so much fill dirt that new oxygen can't get to the roots, they will die, and if the tree develops a fungal disease that is left untreated. How easy it is to make connections to our own cause of root rot! Poor drainage sounds a lot like poor avenues to dispose of negative trauma. If we never learn how to properly cope with dysfunction and pain, we drown in the sorrow of our trauma and develop root rot. The root of a tree that is covered in too much fill dirt is the analogy that I personally resonate with the most. Over time, the enemy piles *so much stuff on us*. If we don't realize and then utilize the power we have in shielding ourselves from the devil's mess, he will put so much stuff on us that we suffocate under the weight of it all. And finally, disease will kill the root of a tree if left untreated. Well, what is the disease that is killing all of humanity at this very moment? Sin. The only treatment for sin is to apply the blood of Jesus to your life! Yes, God's analogies are my favorite. He uses nature to show us the very ways we are damaged and offers the solutions to them all.

With people, it is painful to get to the root of our problems. Our roots are firmly in the ground and buried deep. They are the foundation on which our character was formed, and they affect the health of our entire system—body and mind alike. When those roots are rotten or diseased from childhood trauma or other life-altering events, we interact with the world through an altered perception of reality. This altered perception affects our daily decision-making and choices. This is how I inadvertently leaned into, rather than away from, false idols for years.

When I used to think of false idols, my mind immediately took me to the pages of the Bible. I pictured golden calves and other statues made of choice silver and gold. I shook my head in judgment as I thought of the Israelites worshipping other Gods despite all that God had done for them. To be fair, it's easy to cast judgment when you are privy to the beginning, middle, and end of the journey, right? It's not as easy to spot idol worship in our own lives because we are busy doing the everyday things that take up our time and energy. We are so busy that we don't stop to take inventory of our habits and behaviors often, if ever at all.

CHAPTER 6: THE GOLDEN CALF

If you just read the Bible, God gives us a clear image of idol worship. In biblical times, usually, women introduced their husbands to the gods of their native land and caused the man to commit sin against the one true God. I'm sorry, ladies, but it's true. Solomon, the wisest man to have ever lived, was led astray by his many wives and their false gods. Eve convinced Adam to eat from the only tree God told him to stay away from. Bathsheba and her beauty compelled David, the man after God's own heart, to have an affair and cover it up by sending her husband to the front lines in battle, knowing he would die there! With that thought, let's just grab the remote and press *pause* to appreciate the great impact a woman can have on her husband. Since the fall of man, the woman has been throwing around her influence like candy at a parade. We don't highlight the power of influence we have in a man's life the way that we should. As Uncle Ben told Spiderman (#canyousaymomofboys), "With great power comes great responsibility," and we have a responsibility to use our influence for the good of the kingdom of God and not be a hindrance to the men in our lives. **unpause**

Idol worship in the Bible was much more blatant and easier to see than it is in our lives today. Satan sneaks in idol worship in the most cunning of ways. We need the Holy Spirit to gently show us the ways in which we abuse our freedom to worship. Let me tell you a little story that begins with a chubby little toddler and an angry woman I didn't know.

When my kids were small, I felt angry and on edge a lot. The cheerful, kid-loving woman of my younger days was replaced by a stressed-out, hyper-anxious, analytical stranger the day my first child was born. I didn't know I had transformed right away. It wasn't until later, when my tiny infant became a toddler, that my new identity was fully unmasked. I remember one of the first times my alter ego surfaced. My husband and I had taken our toddler to Cracker Barrel to eat. I had taken him to the bathroom, and when he was finished, I sat him on the counter to help him wash his hands. He had on the most adorable dress shirt, sweater vest, and tiny blue jeans that made him look like a little man. He had slightly long bangs and the most piercing blue eyes that sparkled when he giggled. I was so proud that I had a beautiful child that was dressed well. As I was admiring my tiny tot, an older lady came out of the stall. She began washing her hands, and it wasn't long until she glanced at my toddler and began to speak. No sooner than she began talking, my toddler started barking and growling at this woman! Her face was bewildered and puzzled but not amused. I felt the rush of judgment go down my spine, and my face lit up with heat from embarrassment. I felt so judged by this stranger, and I hated it. Instead of gently rebuking his age-appropriate behavior, I yanked him down from there and swatted his tail. I can hear the harshness of my words as I told him that was a "no-no." My face, still burning with heat, was twisted in a hateful, angry look as I overreacted in a moment of what would be the first of many years of idolatry. My desire for perfection, or the idea of it, trumped everything else. If this same thing happened to me today, I know that I would have laughed out loud at my sweet boy. I wouldn't care one bit what that woman thought, and I would have softly brushed his hair out of his face and gently told him not to bark at people. At least, not most of them.

It hurts my heart to write this memory because it is so painful for me. My soul longs to go back to the days when my children were small and discipline them with the Holy Spirit-filled wisdom I have now. But alas, this is my story, and I can't go back and change what's written on the pages. All I can do is make sure the words that are written from this point forward are dripping with the mercy and grace that is reflective of the great love I was shown when Jesus was hanging on an old, rugged cross for me.

My younger self didn't know half of what she thought she did. She thought if she worked hard to be successful, life would be a piece of cake. She thought that if she got married, graduated college, bought a house, and had a baby, in that order, her life would be perfect. When you spend your childhood experiencing hurt at every turn and are subsequently left alone a lot, you have plenty of time to define what your idea of "perfection" is. Younger me lived life as a victim of circumstance, and unfortunately, that left me with a huge chip on my shoulder. I was determined that I would be and have everything that I wanted as a child, but it was always somehow just out of my reach. When I was younger, I looked around at other girls my age and was in awe that they were living completely different lives than me. I didn't understand why their moms and dads were married. I was envious that they didn't have to worry about the endless list of things that kept me up at night. Would my mom have enough money to pay the electric bill? Would I be able to have the money to turn in for the field trip? Would our car battery die in the pickup line? Why didn't my dad want to take care of us so we didn't have to struggle all the time?

When I went to school, I didn't understand why my friends could have expensive name brand jeans and purses, but that

CHAPTER 6: THE GOLDEN CALF

wasn't an option for me. I wanted to go to gymnastics and dance consistently, but those were luxuries afforded to families with a mom and a dad. I always felt like I never measured up, that no matter how smart, talented, or pretty I was, it would never be enough. When you are looking at life through the jaded lens of resentment, life can seem pretty unfair. The devil further solidified my belief that if I somehow wasn't myself, I would have been born into a life where I had happy circumstances instead of sad ones. I believed that since I was not good enough for even my dad to want to stay with me, why would I be good enough to have the things I yearned for? The hold that Satan began to have on my thought pattern was intense from a young age; don't ever underestimate the desire Satan has for the heart and soul of even the smallest children. Young and old, big and small, he wants them all.

Younger me didn't need anything or anybody and was determined to do it all herself. And even after I gave my life to the Lord, this attitude followed me for years. When I became a mom, I was overwhelmed with joy. I remember sitting and holding my tiny boy and rocking him all the time. He was completely perfect in every way, and I would just stare at his face, trying to store every single detail of it in my memory. I didn't even want to forget what the wrinkles in his tiny forehead looked like or how he scrunched his nose right before he took a bottle. I had never felt such immense love for anyone, and I vowed to do everything in my power to give him the life that I had always wanted. I would give up everything to give him the life he deserved, the perfection that I had been desperately seeking. And that is what I did.

I gave up drinking and going out with friends. I gave up selfish desires and nurtured his instead. I began searching for Jesus in my own personal life. My little infant's innocent face was all the proof I needed of a loving God, and suddenly, I wanted to know Him more. I wanted my baby to not only grow up to have a perfect life but to know a perfect God as well. I began going to church and seeking the Lord. I rededicated my life to God and have been humbly serving Him ever since. I earnestly and honestly loved the Lord with my whole heart. I looked for opportunities and ways to serve Him in all that I did. The trouble was that even in my new believer state, I was carrying around the same luggage from a childhood riddled with trauma. I was seeking perfection in everything, including my relationship with Jesus. I cared about how it looked. I wanted everyone to look at me and say, "Wow! Look how much she loves Jesus! Look at how she takes her child to church so faithfully! Watch how she prays for her husband and his salvation!" It is so embarrassing for me to write these words about myself, but it doesn't make it less true. I spent years in this cycle.

I loved the Lord the best way I knew how. I was going to church and reading my Bible. I had decided that I wanted to follow Jesus, and I knew that for sure. I just didn't know how to stop the destructive cycles and dysfunctional mindset that had shaped my character. I made everything about me. My worship, my acts of service, my prayers, my style of parenting, it was all self-serving. I had inadvertently created this temple of false idols that I worshipped. I worshipped the idea of perfection. Everything I did was done with one goal in mind-to create the illusion of perfection. Idolatry is so damaging because it perverts the very fiber of worship. It takes the act of worship away from a Holy God and places it on things and people that can never satisfy. What a heartbreak our Lord must experience when He sees how we worship things with fervor and praise only he deserves!

I would have never conceded to the idea that I was actively participating in idol worship without God intervening. One afternoon, driving my kids home from school, one of them began to really act out. He was hateful and rude, and I could feel my anger boiling to the surface. I exploded on him right out of the gate, and he was so shocked that he got quiet. No sooner than the stillness filled the air, I heard the Lord say, "You worship your kids' behavior, you know?"

I heard Him tell me that I had made an idol out of my children by trying to control their every move. I worshipped the idea of a perfectly-behaved child. I wrestled with God over this. I tried convincing myself that I wasn't seeking perfection, only respectful children. There isn't anything wrong with disciplining your children. In fact, the Bible tells us that we must discipline them if we love them, just as God disciplines His children. It wasn't the discipline that God had a problem with. My "disciplinary" techniques were a reflection of my heart. My heart was in bad condition. I didn't discipline from a place of holy love, mercy, or grace. I usually disciplined in sinful anger. I would talk in a hateful voice, distort my face into a disapproving glare, and if none of that worked, I would raise my voice and yell. None of this was a reflection of godliness, though, so it was keeping me from reaching the next level with God. I didn't want to believe this was true about myself, so I ignored it for weeks. Despite my best avoidance techniques, God wouldn't let it go. One day, out of the blue, he put someone in my path unexpectedly, and our conversation would help me accept the ugly reality of idol worship in my life. We had a great discussion about raising godly children, and I found myself longing to be the kind of mother she was. She recommended a book that she had just finished, and I ordered it right away. I am ashamed to tell you that I have long since read the book and can't remember the title, but something written within it changed the trajectory of my journey. The author's main purpose of the book was how to steward the hearts of your children well by disciplining them with intention. This was something I had never considered before. Up until this point, I kind of let each day happen to me with whatever it might bring. I considered sibling arguments, endless loads of chores and meals a byproduct of parenting rather than a God-ordained opportunity to minister to my children. After reading this book, I began to see parenting as an active ministry that I was failing at miserably. Had I created tiny false idols, caring more about how things looked and how they acted than stewarding their hearts to love the Lord. The longer I marinated on it, the clearer it became. I was worshipping the idea of perfection more than I was worshipping God. It was just as God had said to me (duh.) I had created tiny false idols in my pursuit of perfection, and they were scattered about in every aspect of my life. I knew I had to clean house.

"Who may ascend the mountain of the Lord? Who may stand in his Holy place? The one with clean hands and a pure heart, who does not trust in an idol or swear by a false God" (Psalm 24:3–4).

When repenting of our sins, it is always a good idea to repent of all sins, known and unknown, for this very reason. While God forgives our sins, both known and unknown, when we ask, unresolved sin that we keep repeating keeps us stuck on the same level. We can't move forward and take a step closer to living a continual life of righteousness if we are stuck on a merry-go-round of repeated sin. It's like a dirty spot on the back of your heavenly garment that you didn't even know was there. We keep washing it clean and then sitting right back down in the exact same spot and getting dirty all over again.

Sometimes, we mislabel behaviors in our lives by taking

the easier road. We say things to excuse our behaviors, like, "This is just how I am." Or "God made me this way." We would do ourselves a favor if we took the road less traveled and identified the real reason we behave in toxic, sinful ways like, "I struggle with the fear of rejection and low self-worth, so I often get angry as a way to force others into molding into my idea of perfection." Ouch. It was P-a-i-n-f-u-l, with a capital P, to admit this truth about myself. I love my children with my whole heart, and the idea that I was inadvertently hurting them because I had unresolved sin in my own life was soul-crushing. I yelled to bully them into submission. And if you are a yeller, that is your goal, too. I realize admitting that sucks. Admitting it was my first step in cleansing myself of false idols. The Lord was faithful in showing me why I wanted to yell. I wanted their behavior to reflect a certain image, and when it didn't, I forced them into quick obedience. I wasn't willing to see them as a work in progress that I could influence and instruct with wisdom and grace. I had one goal in mind all the time, and that was, you guessed it, perfection. Raising my voice was the path of least resistance. I knew that as soon as I raised my voice, they would get quiet because when someone raises their voice at you, it is intimidating. And do you know where I learned this little tidbit of information about the effects of yelling? My dad.

When God works inside of you, it is messy! But He is faithful to weave every single moment that has happened, past and present, into one beautiful masterpiece if you'll let Him. He had to reveal to me that I was serving false idols not only for my own benefit but for that of my children and future generations. He helped me get to the root cause of this particular sin by taking me down memory lane. My sister and I would go see our dad for two weeks in the summer. My dad has two brothers and a sister, and they would all make sure their kids were there at the same time. My cousins, my sister, and I would be left home with our grandmother during the day, and at night, it was common for all the adults to either leave or drink and play poker, so we were alone then, too. The older girls in the family, me included, were in charge of babysitting the younger cousins and also household chores. My dad would come home, either upset from a long day at work or already drunk, and inevitably, he would get angry about something. He wouldn't yell at my sister, but he had no problem yelling at me. I didn't realize it until the Lord revealed it to me, but every single time he would get angry, he would shout, "G** d*** it, Christina!" His tone would go deep, and his voice boomed. He would snarl his nose in a disgusted look and grit his teeth. He was terrifying. This always resulted in me hunkering down and going into survival mode. I would mentally curl into a ball and cry, and outwardly, I would just do what needed to be done in an effort to please this man I could never seem to please. My existence seemed to bother him. I learned that if you just do what someone is asking you to do quickly, the anger would usually simmer quickly.

As I grew up, when I felt out of place, felt inadequate, or made a mistake, I would hear his voice in my head repeating, "G** d*** it, Christina!"

Satan had a field day with this. He would add to this phrase every time.

"You are incapable of doing anything right!"

"You are literally a screw-up!"

"You will *never* be enough!"

As I walked away from the false idol of perfection, I had to leave this voice behind, too. It had taught me that yelling equals submission, and hearing it always resolidified my belief that I was unworthy of love.

Maybe you are worshipping false idols, too. Where do you put all your emphasis and time? Is it a job or promotion? Maybe it's a lifestyle you are trying to upkeep. Do you put your time and money into acquiring material things? Now would be a good time for self-reflection. What is it that you *treasure*? The pursuit of righteousness will cause you to let go of anything that stands between you and the Lord.

"For where your treasure is, there your heart will be also" (Matthew 6:21).

CHAPTER 7:
The Sin We're In: People-Pleasing Edition

> "If I were still trying to please people, I would not be a servant of Christ."
>
> GALATIANS 1:10

If you are, or have ever been, a people-pleaser, take heart! You are in good company. When Paul was addressing the church at Galatia, he said this:

"Am I now trying to win the approval of human beings, or of God? Or am I trying to please people? If I were still trying to please people, I would not be a servant of Christ" (Galatians 1:10).

That tiny yet important word "still" serves as hope for us all. That five-letter word makes Paul suddenly more relatable than he was before. Paul was admitting that he was a people-pleaser at some point in his life. The language he used was specific and purposeful. He was telling his audience that although he used to worry about the opinions of others, he was able to overcome it by fully committing his life to Christ. Paul's admission serves as a powerful reminder: If you want to serve God wholeheartedly, be honest with yourself about your shortcomings. An honest examination of your heart will show you what you must overcome. And make no mistake, people-pleasing *is* something you need to overcome.

Labeling someone a people-pleaser is a nice way to say that the sin that rules their life is that of idol worship. I would go so far as to say that the need to please others isn't rooted in kindness. That's not to say that people-pleasers aren't naturally tender-hearted people. I absolutely think they are tender-hearted and kind. This is exactly the characteristic that left them vulnerable to attack. People-pleasers are wounded people. They either suffered loss, heartache, or circumstances that were out of their control during the formative years. In response to that circumstance, people-pleasers develop unique coping mechanisms.

The driving force behind this need is calculated anticipation. By controlling what others do, we can anticipate the outcome and prepare ourselves accordingly. This is a form of self-preservation for those who often had life-altering events thrown at them unexpectedly. They worship control. Of course, no one would ever admit to this, but in the back of their mind, they have decided that they trust themselves to control situations more than they trust God. This is how this form of people-pleasing is sinful. This is also the root cause of my need to please others. I wanted complete control of the situations and people around me so I never had to experience the deep pain that came when my dad abruptly left and my mom experienced the loss of her vision. In reality, though, it is impossible to control everything and everyone around me, and so I was always left feeling exhausted, burned out, and bitter from the futile attempts. Maybe this is where you fall as well. They have a deep need to appease everyone they meet. They crave acceptance from people and want to be liked. They want to be included. A people-pleaser will begrudgingly do themselves a disservice and lie about their own feelings to avoid potential conflict. They often have trouble setting appropriate boundaries with those around them. They want to walk through life on untroubled waters, and accomplishing that is much easier when the people around you are pleasantly floating around on water that is still. On the surface, people-pleasers look like they lack the backbone to stand up to others and make their voice known for fear of rejection. And for some people-pleasers, maybe this is true to an extent. Until God told me otherwise, I believed that to be true for me. Once I began seeking the Lord, asking Him to show me why I desperately desired the approval of others, He was faithful to deliver. Simply put, pleasing people was a way to control the unknowns around me. Yes, at the root of my desire to please others was a need for total control. I thought that total control of the world around me was more worthy of my time and energy than pleasing God.

> "Isaiah said these things because he saw Jesus' glory and spoke of him. Yet at the same time many even among the leaders believed in him. But because of the Pharisees they would not openly acknowledge their faith for fear they would be put out of the synagogue; for they loved human praise more than praise from God."
>
> JOHN 12:41–43

CHAPTER 7: THE SIN WE'RE IN: PEOPLE-PLEASING EDITION

The people-pleaser will strive to control the attitudes, reactions, and behaviors of everyone in their sphere of influence. Yes, on top of idol worship, people-pleasers don't have the faith in God that is necessary to stand on His Word. People pleasers make everything about themselves rather than about God. Instead of allowing God to be in control, they desire control. I know it is hard to hear. It's hard for me to even write because, in the back of my mind, I am afraid you will be offended by what I have said (I am a former people-pleaser, after all). But since I now know better than what I was doing before, it would be a disservice for me not to pass along the wisdom I gained through painful experience. I want you to walk victoriously toward heaven with the insight and knowledge that comes from overcoming the root cause of the sins you stay stuck in. The harsh truth is that you just can't serve them both. You cannot ride the fence and try to tend to the flesh and the spirit. You know this, though. You *have* to know that the desire to constantly please people isn't holy because of the fruit it produces.

When you are constantly striving for human acceptance and approval, your thoughts are dominated by anxiety, obsessive tendencies, worry, and doubt. Your inner voice might sound something like this:

"Did I make her mad? She is going to hate me."

"Should I have said that? That was such a dumb thing to say."

"If I say no to her invitation, she will stop liking me/inviting me/thinking of me."

"If I don't sacrifice myself and my beliefs to tend to their needs, I am not a good person. A good person never makes others inconvenienced."

"Is that post she made about me? Did I do something to her and not know it? I should call her and ask her if I made her upset."

"I want to tell her she hurt my feelings, but if I confront her, we might not be friends anymore."

"I want to tell my friend that what she is doing is sinful, but she will reject me and think I am being judgmental, so I won't say anything at all."

All of these thoughts were normal for me to have on any given day. Honestly, I could have had all of these thoughts in a one-hour time frame if my anxiety was heightened or I was already stressed. It never took much for my mind to begin riding the roller coaster of emotions that come with trying to make sure everyone is happy all of the time. I walked on eggshells around people that had no idea the shells were even on the ground. They didn't throw the eggshells down and create a fragile environment. I was perfectly capable of doing that myself. I would randomly assign feelings and needs to others based on what my feelings were that day. If I hadn't been reading my Bible and praying like I should, destructive thought patterns multiplied at rapid speed. If I was engaged in any kind of confrontational situation with family or friends, I assigned those feelings to all those relationships in my life. I believed that if I was having a disagreement with one person, every relationship I had was under attack. Paranoia and perfectionism would set in as I tried to be extra accommodating to everyone else. I falsely believed that if one person was upset with me, it was because I had let my guard down and tried to be myself rather than please everyone else. The idea that confrontation, misunderstandings, and disagreements naturally happen from time to time wasn't even an option I considered. Instead, I would mentally beat myself up and become hyper-intentional in my efforts to make people happy. This created complete misery and chaos in my mind. Everything I felt and did produced fruits that left me rotten inside. The torment and exhaustion that comes with trying to be everything for everyone is extraordinary. It's like being in a boat with holes in the floorboard. You are trying to fill up buckets of water and dump them out before everyone you know and love drowns, but the water comes so fast, you can't keep up. You wear yourself out trying until, eventually, the whole boat sinks. *It is impossible to please everyone, and trying to do so is a sin.* And what does sin cause? Death.

"For the wages of sin is death; but the gift of our God is eternal life through Jesus Christ our Lord" (Romans 6:23).

If you can admit that you suffer from the sin of people-pleasing, congratulations! Realizing that you sin in ways that don't always feel sinful is a huge part of your journey to righteousness. And for what it's worth, I am super proud of you. What's a woman to do after accepting the reality of the sin she is in? I'm so glad you asked. You are now at an extremely pivotal point in your walk with the Lord. You can either trust God to help you figure out why you have a deep desire to please others, or you can try to figure it out on your own. Only one of those options will give you lasting relief. I know this from experience.

For years, I tried to tackle it on my own. I would give myself pep talks and read self-help books. I would listen to podcasts from professionals trying to coach others on how to not care what anyone else thought. I took all the advice I could get. I would try different techniques and approaches to situations, but nothing felt natural. I took into consideration the fact that nothing feels natural at first, but this feeling was different than that. When I used the suggestions from the world, I was always left feeling like a fake. It made me feel uneasy because I had to calculate and analyze my every action and reaction in an effort to test out a new approach. I would eventually slip right back into old patterns and behaviors because although I was trying to change, I hadn't given it to the Lord. The world will always yield to the world. I 0/10 recommend tackling the people-pleasing giant with the world's approach.

When the world's approach failed me time and again, I finally decided to take it to God. I was at the end of myself in a lot of ways. I was seeking God more than I ever had, and for the first time, I began to loathe the fact that I craved the acceptance of others. I hated that I was afraid to take a stand on biblical issues like abortion because I didn't want to upset people that might push back. I began to detest my sin so profoundly that I retreated into myself. If I didn't have to be around people at all, then I wouldn't have to worry about pleasing them. In theory, this seemed like a good fix, but it is not practical for daily application. Not to mention that this method only put a band-aid on the wound instead of treating it and eradicating it completely. As my soul grew closer to the Lord, I knew avoidance wasn't the answer. My heart could no longer handle the sins that I kept repeating as if on a loop. I sought the Lord and asked Him to show me *why* I had this need for acceptance and approval. If I could just understand where it started, I would know what to pray against.

"I confess my iniquity. I am troubled by my sin" (Psalm 38:18).

The first thing He revealed to me was what I had already shared at the beginning of this book. My dad leaving our family when I was just a small girl fundamentally changed who I was growing up to be. I always knew on some level that the issues I had with acceptance were rooted in the loss of my family, particularly my dad. I just didn't understand that there were other moments in my life that reinforced this behavior that had to be addressed as well.

My dad got sick and had a massive stroke in his 30s. He suffered short-term memory loss and paralysis on his right side. Although sickness is never good, I credit this traumatic event in his life as being the reason he gave his heart to the Lord. When my dad got sick, he couldn't go out and drink or party anymore. His "friends" quit coming around, and his life began to be nothing like it had been in the past. It took a long time, but eventually, he got his heart right with the Lord and became the father and papaw that my sister and I had desperately desired. If our kids have a game, he is in the stands cheering them on. If they celebrate a success, he is right there with them. If they experience loss, he feels their pain as if it is his own. The glory of the Lord changed my dad completely. He just got his attention with a stroke that slowed him down and drowned out the noise.

My dad has long since apologized, and to this day, he says his biggest regret is leaving his family. In fact, my dad was able to realize that his father had hurt him, too, and he never learned how to be the dad that we deserved. He was once a small child who needed his dad, too, and was left with the bitter taste of alcoholism, adultery, and destruction. He only mimicked the cycle that had raised him with his family. My heart began to soften toward him when I realized that he also suffered from childhood trauma. The trouble was that even after our relationship was restored and he apologized, I was still left with the damage. I began to pray that God would rid me of the toxic behaviors I had developed, and I also began to ask Him to show me anything unknown that was hindering me.

God was faithful to bring memories to my mind that were painful to face, things I hadn't thought about in years. One of those memories revealed what I believe to be the catalyst that launched my controlling tendencies into overdrive. God brought to my remembrance a time at my dad's house when I was ten years old. My sister and I would go visit my dad every other weekend and for two weeks in the summer. It was always hectic because they all lived with my nanny, and they would all get their children for visitation at the same time. On the one hand, this was great because I loved being with my cousins. We would stay up all night long playing Nintendo 64 and watching movies that my mom would never let us watch. We played outside all day and had a barn that had animals, rope swings, and endless fun.

On the other hand, the alcohol and partying didn't stop because we were there and it never ended well. My dad, my papaw, and his brothers would stay up all night drinking and playing cards. Occasionally, they wanted my cousins and me to play cards with the adults. They liked to make us have adult consequences if we lost a round because it was funny for them. For example, if you were the loser, sometimes you had to stand up, open your palm flat, and let one of the adult men flip the palm of your hand with a rubber band. It might not sound like a big deal, but when all the kids are twelve and under, it was a dreaded punishment that always hurt. Other times, you would be forced to drink an entire glass of water quickly or have hot sauce poured into your mouth. It was humiliating because no matter your reaction, all the adults would laugh and make fun of you and dare you to cry. One night, I was told to come play, but I declined. I was writing my boyfriend a letter and really wanted to finish the letter. They left me alone initially and let me write. I couldn't believe that I got to do what I wanted to do, and it didn't come with a consequence! I finished the letter and was about to fold it when my uncle came stumbling into the room and ripped it out of my hand. He took off toward the kitchen, and before I could get up, I heard him reading it out loud. The table of men erupted in laughter and immediately started mocking things I had written. Ten-year-olds can be pretty ridiculous, and I had started the letter by saying, "Hey, love bunny." Gah. That was actually embarrassing for me to type out because it sounded so dumb. Regardless, this is what ten-year-old me had settled on and was happy with. The rest of the time I was at my dad's, my uncles, cousins, and papaw called me love bunny. I was so mortified that I never wanted to feel that way again, under any circumstance. Without realizing it, that moment in the kitchen solidified my desire to please people so I could control how they interacted with me. If I would have played cards like they asked, I would have been spared the humiliation that came with doing what I wanted. When God showed me this memory from childhood, so many dots of my past were connected. It's important to note that this process didn't take place overnight. It was painful for me to relive certain memories, and when the pain would hit, I would avoid any progress for days or weeks rather than feel pain. If you ask God to show you the root causes of your pain, be ready and willing to deal with memories that will be unpleasant, difficult, and uncomfortable. Had I known this upfront, I might not have been so shocked when the pain

I hadn't experienced in years felt fresh and new, causing my progress to be prolonged.

I don't have any research to back this up (although I am certain I could find some if I tried), but I feel qualified to assume a couple of things because of my own life experience. I believe that when something traumatic happens to a child, the brain hides that memory away deep in the recesses of the mind. As a child grows, the memory stays buried so well that the conscious mind doesn't even remember that it happened. The child grows into an adult with big problems (think anxiety, the fear of rejection, the need for approval, depression, etc.), and instead of understanding that the negative quality is a byproduct of an event or series of events from their past, they take on that trait as part of who they are as a person. Like they were hardwired to have crippling anxiety and depression from birth or something. What if we accept these traits not as our identity but as something negative we need to be freed from? Anything that keeps us from walking in the victory and authority that God has for us is definitely something that doesn't need to stay in our lives. God is able to take what is broken and restore it to something more beautiful than before. God *is* the God of restoration, after all. Restoration means taking something old and run-down and making it new again. If you will ask Him, God is faithful to perform a complete factory reset in your life. He can take the traits that bring sickness to the body and soul and restore you to the person He intended for you to be.

To help you more clearly see how this process works, let's examine an analogy. Before you restore a run-down property, you must repair whatever issues were causing it to be run down in the first place. If you don't take care of those things, they will resurface and cause damage again. For example, if you have water damage and mold from years of leaking pipes, it will do no good to replace the drywall and flooring if you don't fix the leak. Eventually, that leak will cause the same destruction it did before. The same thing is true with your soul. Whatever it is that caused you to experience the deep need to control things around you has to be addressed. If you don't address that directly, no matter how much time you spend in therapy, how many self-help books you read, or how many podcasts you listen to, you will still be left with the same destructive patterns and behaviors that will eventually hinder any progress you try to make. Commit yourself to the Lord today and earnestly pray that He would show you the root cause of your need to control the situations around you. He will show you, and then He will graciously help you to heal from what hurt you. If Jesus wasn't a people-pleaser, then you don't need to be one, either. And if the sin that you stay stuck in isn't people-pleasing, that's okay, too. You and God know the sins that keep you tied and bound. No matter the sin, God can show you the root cause of it and wipe it clean if you'll trust Him with it.

CHAPTER 8:
Freedom Fighter

Before you can become a victorious woman in Christ, you must learn how to be a warrior. Victories aren't just given; they are earned on the battlefield, right? The gift of salvation is freely given to you and me by a loving and merciful Savior. But if you are looking for the joy, victory, and peace that comes from serving God, you have to wage war on your enemy. Victory and righteous authority that sends demons back into the pits of hell is not found anywhere but on the battlefield. Are you ready to learn how to fight out of the bondage that Satan has been keeping you in? Put on your armor and pick up your sword, sister. Victory is within reach!

The sin that held me in bondage for years was the worship of false idols. That manifested itself in many different areas of my life. Ultimately, I wanted to please people more than I wanted to please God, and that made me hyper-focused on control. After I identified it, it didn't just disappear. I had to be set free from that stronghold the enemy had on me. And a stronghold is hard to break. Mostly because, well, it's a stronghold that the enemy has on your life. To break free, I had to go to war! I'm a lover, not a fighter, so war was difficult and terrifying for me at first. It might sound terrifying to you, too. But I am living proof that you can fight and you can *win*! I am a girly girl through and through. You know how everyone has a fight or flight response to danger? Mine has always been flight. So trust me when I say that God can take even the weakest warrior and transform her into a force to be reckoned with.

You can't go into war unless you have studied your enemy. Well, technically, I guess you *can* go fight against an unknown enemy, but why would you want to? If you plan on winning the war, you got to know the characteristics of the enemy. You've got to understand why they are fighting the battle against you. Not only that, but you also have to understand what lengths your adversary will go to in an effort to win the war. To make certain of your victory, it's not enough to just know who you are fighting against. If you want to win, you've got to study the enemy's tactics. If you can understand the strategies being used against you, then you can prepare a counter-offense before the enemy makes the first move. The more you know about your enemy, the less likely you are to be caught in an unexpected attack, right? Wars are won with strategy, careful analysis of the enemy, and the strength and courage to carry out the mission to the end. So, what does all of this have to do with your walk with the Lord? I'm so glad you asked.

One of my favorite songs is called "I'm On the Battlefield for My Lord," written by E.V. Banks and Sylvanna Bell. The lyrics are a beautiful representation of the battlefield you and I walk onto every day of our lives. I encourage you to take a few minutes and listen to it.

The song is short, and the lyrics are simplistic, but it delivers a message that applies to all believers. The writer starts out by recognizing the condition they were in when God found them: idle and alone. Idle, when used as an adjective, can mean that a person is lazy and avoids work or that something is pointless and without purpose. As a verb, it means to spend time doing nothing. Wow. There's a whole sermon packed in the words "idle sinner," but you get the point. When God calls you into His army, you are practically useless and unfit to fight. You have been spending time doing nothing of importance or value for the Lord, let alone training for battle.

Then God calls the singer to walk with Him. The moment he takes God's hand, he walks directly onto the piece of ground where the war is fought—*the battlefield*! That was quick! No training, no time to study. The attacks from the enemy start right away. How is a new Christian supposed to fight in a battle he knows virtually nothing about? The short answer is that the enemy will probably gain some ground. The writer alludes to this with the line, "I lost my flag in battle." In war, a battle flag represents a military unit, and when you lose your flag, the enemy camp has taken it and won a victory over you. Losing your battle flag means that you were defeated during a particular battle, and losing it damages the morale of the troops. When you first begin serving the Lord, it is easy to feel like the enemy has taken your flag and gained ground. It's hard to fight when you don't really know how! That's why *I love the next line*! "My staff is in my hand." Guess who else had a staff in his hand? Okay, fine. I'll tell you. It was Moses. Moses who was abandoned in basket because his mother had no choice. Moses who was found and raised by none other than Pharoah's daughter despite Pharoah being the one who ordered all the baby boys be killed. Moses who God set apart for a purpose. Moses who didn't want to do what God was asking him to do because he stuttered when he spoke. Moses, the one who led the Israelites out of Egypt. Moses who etched the Ten Commandments on the stone tablet after a visitation from God. Yep. Moses had a staff that he held in his hand, too.

"Now the Lord had said to Moses in Midian, 'Go back to Egypt, for all those who wanted to kill you are dead.' So Moses took his wife and sons, put them on a donkey and started back to Egypt. And he took the staff of God in his hand" (Exodus 4:19–20).

God wanted Moses to know that He had given him powers to perform signs and wonders in front of Pharoah, and the staff served as his assurance of God's presence and power. It doesn't matter if it feels like the enemy has captured your flag; God's presence and power go with you everywhere, and that will sustain you as you press on to the promised land.

The final lyrics explain just what we are fighting for. You are fighting for Jesus until He returns and takes you on to your heavenly reward! That's something worth fighting for. Notice the lyrics tell you that when He comes to take you home, take off your armor and put on your robe and crown. All warriors needed to be suited up with the armor of God from head to toe, regardless of their experience in battle. Are you suited up and ready to fight? If not, the enemy is sure to launch a sneak attack, and the next thing you know, you are being held captive, a prisoner of war. If you find yourself in bondage, bound by chains of despair, there is hope for you yet! Freedom is within reach and a promised reward.

Make no mistake; you have the most cunning, evil enemy that humanity has ever known. Prior to you getting saved, the devil has laid claim to you. He is the Lord of your life, and he governs your thoughts and mind. Unsaved people don't have to be evil to be under Satan's dominion. The devil is no respecter of person. He will hold *anyone* hostage, sinner and saved alike. It's a hard pill to swallow, but if God isn't the Lord of your life, then, by default, Satan is. Jesus even says it in the Book of Matthew, chapter 12. He says, **"Whoever is not with me is against me, and whoever does not gather with me scatters."** Jesus makes it perfectly clear. If you aren't on His side, you are on the side of His enemy. And sis, that ain't good. The devil doesn't "take it easy" on you when you are his, though. The devil just attacks you differently when you aren't actively serving God. He's already holding you as a prisoner of war, and as long as you are comfortable fumbling around in the darkness of your cell, he knows your fate is death.

My saved sisters in Christ aren't exempt from the devil's schemes either. On the day that you became a child of God, the devil put a bullseye on your back. He positioned demons at the ready, waiting to pounce and attack you with all of hell's fury. Yep, with the acceptance of Christ as your Savior, you position yourself on the front lines of a warzone. Hell's army wants to drag you back into enemy territory where they can continue to hold you hostage with your favorite sin. I'd love to tell you that once a woman finds Jesus, she walks out of her bondage and experiences freedom, but that isn't the case with most of the people I know. It wasn't the case for me, either. The difficulty women experience as they search for the daily freedoms in serving a living God is two-fold. First, many women simply don't know how to fight spiritual warfare. They get saved, and then all of a sudden, it seems like everything in their lives is falling apart. The money gets tight, they argue with their spouse, a child acts out. Just because you are inexperienced in warfare doesn't mean the devil gives you time to get up to speed. Nope, he immediately begins launching attacks and tries to wear you out and keep you too discouraged to learn to fight.

It sure would be nice if getting saved came with an instruction manual. Oh, wait. It *does*! God's holy Word lays out the roadmap for battle and tells you exactly how to counter the enemy and keep him from setting up camp in your life. The trouble is that most women don't know where to start, and if they do start, they get overwhelmed by the size and complexity of the Scripture. The overwhelming feeling of not knowing what or how to tackle the Scripture leads to burnout and, eventually, avoidance. Instead of reading the Bible, they will find other ways to fill their time. Maybe a quick TikTok or Facebook reel with a micro-sermon. Anything to avoid having to read and try to interpret the Word. This leads to the next difficulty that saved women face. After the devil sees that you are worn out from fighting, he drags you right back into captivity. It's familiar there in your cell, and you like the comfort that being in captivity brings. So you settle back into your bondage and are content to be there.

I know, I know, you are probably thinking that you would never be comfortable wallowing around in captivity! You would have the good sense to know that the devil has taken hold of you and thrown you into a little dark cell of despair. But what if you were so occupied that you didn't even realize he had closed the door and locked you in? Let me explain. Satan knows what your weaknesses are. He knows the first thing you turn to when you feel a little stress. Maybe it's food. Or a flirty relationship at work. Maybe it's a pill or alcohol, maybe sexual perversions or multiple partners. Perhaps it's something else. Only you and God know what it is. Oh, wait. That's not exactly true. There is one more party who knows what you do in the darkness. (Duh, obviously, he would since he is the one who put you in the darkness in the first place, but I digress.) Everyone always warns people to behave because God sees what they do even when no one else does, but nobody warns us that the devil sees it, too. That's scriptural, sis.

> "Be alert and of sober mind. Your enemy the devil prowls around like a roaring lion looking for someone to devour."
>
> 1 PETER 5:8

The Bible tells you that the devil is literally roaming around the earth looking for someone he can consume whole. And so what do you think the devil uses to keep you comfortable groaning around in captivity? He consumes you by throwing in your favorite temptation for you to gorge yourself on. That's

CHAPTER 8: FREEDOM FIGHTER

right. He will use what your carnal soul craves and throw you just enough to keep you satisfied. A "fun" sexual encounter that you knew was wrong, a few too many drinks on a girl's night out. A schedule packed so full of places to be and things to do that there is no time to sit in the presence of God. A pill to help you take the edge off. Food that you hope will fill the void in your soul. Without Jesus, humanity has no hope. And when you are being held in bondage and captivity without hope, all efforts to escape seem futile. Rescue seems impossible. When you have reached your point of exhaustion, life feels like too great a burden to bear, as even the ground beneath your feet seems to be falling away. This is where the devil wants to keep you! He likes you miserable and hopeless. Before long, numbness sets in, and the things that once bothered you don't seem to bother you anymore. Numb to the hurt. Numb to the pain. Numb to any emotion at all. Darkness puts your life on autopilot as you move meaninglessly from one moment to the next.

Sometimes, though, despite being in darkness and despair, something will happen that is so significant it causes the person to be jolted into a sudden state of alertness. Once alert, things began to look and feel a little differently. Autopilot is turned off, and you look at the world around you with a new perspective.

New perspectives are often exciting, and with excitement comes hope. And hope anchors the soul (Hebrews 6:19). When the soul is anchored in hope, suddenly things don't seem so unsure. You can reach out for Jesus and step out of captivity. What once felt hopeless and like unsteady ground feels solid and sure beneath your feet. Jesus meets you on the very first step and breaks the chains keeping you bound! The rescue mission has been initiated! Your Savior has come and taken you by the hand, leading you to everlasting life!

Several years ago, my family and I went on a long road trip. My husband had been driving and desperately needed a nap, so I hopped in the driver's seat to dutifully take my turn. The car was quiet because my family was asleep. The longer I drove on the interstate, the more hypnotizing it became. I found myself being lulled to sleep by the familiar sound of the tires on the wide-open road in front of me. It's easy to fall asleep at the wheel when the conditions are just right. Suddenly, I found myself barreling toward construction and closed lanes at a dangerous speed. Instantly, I had to become alert and slam on my brakes to keep from hitting the cones in the road. I glanced in the rearview, made a panic move into the right lane, and tried to slow my racing heart. The impending danger and roadblocks caused me to awaken from my mental sleep. Even more, the further I got from the construction, the more my mind raced with scary thoughts. What if I had been a few seconds slower in my reaction? Would I have pummeled into the construction and hurt someone as a result? Even though I was driving a vehicle with everyone I love inside, I allowed the level of comfort I was experiencing to supersede the potential danger. I let my guard down even though I knew how grave the consequences of that could be. And that's how our relationship is with the Lord sometimes, too.

In the hour that followed this event, the Lord began to reveal His thoughts to me. I heard Him say, "If you aren't alert and aware of what is going on around you, just like the construction snuck up on you, the devil will sneak up and try to bring destruction on you and your house! Are you asleep in your spirit? Do you need to wake up and refix your focus on me?" This message from the Lord impacted me so profoundly that I think of it and tell others about it as often as I can. The devil is out to destroy you, and if you allow yourself to stay comfortable in the familiarity of your favorite sin, he will pop up and attack you when you least expect it. The results could lead to spiritual death. Thankfully, when you are a saved woman who had fallen asleep at the wheel, God will send poignant and powerful reminders that shake up your spirit and refocus your vision.

When I retell this event, I make a point to tell people that the Lord was so gracious to me and allowed me to see the light. God is such a good Father to His children and cares for us in the most uniquely perfect ways. He waited until I got away from the routine of my everyday life and the distractions were taken away to speak directly to my spirit. I had been going through the motions in my spiritual life and was stuck on autopilot, driving in darkness. The devil couldn't make me bad anymore, so instead, he kept me busy. I was constantly moving but never doing anything of great spiritual value. I'd be busy taking kids to and from sports, volunteering at school and church, I'd fill my days with extended family obligations and events; I was up-to-date on the latest fitness and health craze (my early thirties consisted entirely of pilates, a juicer, and essential oils. Yes, I was one of *those women*). Anything to fill my schedule and make me feel important. I am a recovering people-pleaser, as you know. I thrived on a busy schedule. The thing about constantly moving, though, is that when you finally sit down for the night, your body is overwhelmed with exhaustion. I would sit down to read my Bible after the kids went to bed and wake up two hours later with a kink in my neck from sleeping sitting straight up. I'd stumble to bed without reading a single chapter and wake up the next day to do it all again. I didn't realize my spiritual self was on autopilot until the Lord revealed it to me.

This wasn't the first time the Lord had set me free from the captivity and bondage Satan was keeping me in. If you remember, I had a much darker period in my life where I didn't feel of any value to anyone on earth. Demons of darkness and depression taunted me night and day, and I didn't know how to fight in either the spiritual or earthly realm. Instead, I put myself on autopilot and existed merely for the comfort of others. The Lord, in His loving kindness, allowed me to total my car and snap me back into a state of spiritual and mental alertness. The day that I wrecked and then confessed the intrusive thoughts that I had been having to my husband, God opened the door for me to leave the prison Satan kept me shackled in. Just verbalizing the darkness that had been dwelling in my mind for a long time to another believer in Christ felt like freedom. The devil will have you keeping dark feelings a secret, and he will do it under the guise of shame and judgment. That's because he knows the moment you confess and ask Jesus for help, He is faithful to rescue you! I cannot stress to you enough to tell another trusted believer in Christ when you are having dark thoughts and let them pray with you and offer encouragement. You'd be surprised at how receptive your fellow believers are and how much they want to help you! If nothing else, remember that we are made to commune together. It's scriptural!

"For where two or three are gathered in my name, I am there among them" (Matthew 18:20).

"As iron sharpens iron, so one person sharpens another" (Proverbs 27:17).

As awesome as freedom feels, you must remember that the second you step out of your prison, your feet land on the front lines of battle. Your escape from Satan's snares makes you an active target for the devil. The further you walk with Jesus, the more alert hell and all hell's demons become. They understand that there is a war being waged, and the prize is souls. They want your soul, and they want it in bondage. And so the devil, being evil in all his ways, launches a full-on war.

Our society has created this image of the devil and his demons like they are some kind of bumbling, stumbling, dumb fools who can't do anything right. TV and movies have romanticized them. This couldn't be further from the truth. The devil and his demons are dangerous! They seek to kill, steal, and destroy! You don't believe in demons? Well, this is awkward. I hate to tell you like this, but demons are the devil's fallen angel army. Just what did you think happened to the third of the angels that fell from heaven when Lucifer led the rebellion?

"Then another sign appeared in heaven: an enormous red dragon with seven heads and ten horns and seven crowns on its heads. Its tail swept a third of the stars out of the sky and flung them to earth" (Revelation 12:3–4).

Demons were once angels who chose to become an enemy of God. Still not convinced?

"For our struggle is not against flesh and blood, but against the rulers, against the authorities, against the powers of this dark world and against the spiritual forces of evil in this heavenly realm" (Ephesians 6:12).

Demonic forces, or demons, are the rulers, the authorities, and the powers of this dark world. And at any rate, they are your solemn enemy, so you better get on board and learn how to become a worthy and victorious adversary lest they torment you the rest of your time on this earth.

"The thief comes only to steal, kill and destroy; I have come that they may have life, and have it to the full" (John 10:10).

It's a literal warzone out there, ladies. Do you know which side you're on? Or have you picked a side at all? In case there's any question, let's look at the qualities of the leaders on either side of this battle. Imagine that God and the devil are the leading commanders in opposing armies. Satan's main objective is to rob you, destroy your life, and then kill you, while God sent Jesus to give you a fulfilling, prosperous life. While God feeds His soldiers manna, the devil feeds his captors lies. While God covers and protects His troops, the devil catches them in a snare. Satan leads his captors straight into destruction while God gives His warriors everlasting life. While God trades beauty for ashes, Satan is hell-bent on leaving you in a heap of broken ruins. God quite literally breathes life into us time and time again while Satan tries to suffocate us under the weight of his kingdom. I want to follow God into battle because He loves me and His plans for me are good. I bet the bank that you want to follow Him, too. If you haven't drawn a line in the sand yet as to whom you serve, do it today. You must choose which side you are on, and then you must fight.

> "Now fear the Lord and serve him with all faithfulness. Throw away the gods your ancestors worshiped beyond the Euphrates River and in Egypt, and serve the Lord. But if serving the Lord seems undesirable to you, then choose for yourselves this day whom you will serve, whether the gods your ancestors served beyond the Euphrates, or the gods of the Amorites, in whose land you are living. But as for me and my household, we will serve the Lord."
>
> JOSHUA 24:14–15

The second Book of Timothy, chapter 2:24–26, illustrates the different approaches of both God and Satan with regard to you.

> "And the Lord's servant must not be quarrelsome but kind to everyone, able to teach, patiently enduring evil, correcting his opponents with gentleness. God may perhaps grant them repentance leading to a knowledge of truth, and they may come to their senses and escape the snare of devil, after being captured by him to do his will."

Did you catch that last part? Not only does the devil catch you in a trap, but he forces you to be an instrument of evil. Satan is out to steal, kill, and destroy. That means when he has you in bondage, he is using you to support those causes. Oy vey. That's enough to make a grown woman sick to her stomach. Most of you would never knowingly bring destruction to others unless the devil convinced you that you were justified in doing his deeds. The devil is a liar and the father of lies, so you can bet your britches that he can convince you of anything he wants if your guard is down. I can see that face you are making right now. You don't believe that the devil can convince you that your actions are justified? Well, let's throw a few scenarios around that might make you a believer.

CHAPTER 8: FREEDOM FIGHTER

You know that friend you have who was a mistress and eventually became a wife? The one who said her boyfriend hated his wife because she was controlling and inattentive to his needs? The one who told you it was okay because he was in the process of leaving her anyway. Who does she serve? It's easy to tell by looking at her fruits. Her justification causes the destruction of a marriage, perhaps a family with children. It breaks one of God's commandments. The byproduct of her "finding love" causes years of heartbreak and trauma for the spouse who was abandoned and the children left in the wreckage. Yet our society has normalized it so much that no one really bats an eye when it happens. Satan's dominion is this earth, and the fabric of society is stitched together by his web of lies.

What about the woman who gossips about her friends with others when they aren't around? You know, she is in your friend group, and she spills the tea and then follows up with, "Now, I'm only telling y'all this so you can pray." Everybody knows good and well she is telling you this so you can all secretly judge the other person and feel superior to them, but nobody wants to talk about that (where's that Kermit the Frog meme when you need it? Close your eyes and visualize Kermit sipping his tea and staring out the window 'cause that's the meme I would for sure use to drive this point on home). She probably also quotes Scripture every now and then and is the first to drop the praying hands emoji in the comments when you ask for prayer. But her fruits tell the story of who tends her garden. When she gossips, she cuts down the person she is talking about. When she tells that one little secret, she is doing the exact opposite of what God requires of her. God tells us in 1 Peter 4: 8 what to do when you know about gossip and the sins of another. **"Above all, love each other deeply, because love covers a multitude of sins."** God wants you to cover it, not throw the covers off and show the whole world what you know about another. The devil convinces people that they are just telling their friends so others can pray about it. In reality, he's got people slinging untruths and slander and heaping shame on others in the process.

What about those drinks on Friday night that you have with friends? You know, because you just drink socially, not to get drunk. The world has made it look glamorous for people to sit around and casually drink to unwind. But the world cleverly leaves out the part about the dad that stays too long at the bar on Friday night and misses his daughter's recital. Or the mom who just wanted to have a few drinks to take the edge off, but her kids saw her tipsy. In the short term, the devil makes it feel okay because he tells you that you are human and humans make mistakes. While that is true, some mistakes and heartbreak can be avoided entirely with a little forward spiritual thinking. The long-term implications of just a few drinks are seen in the generations that will follow in the footsteps of their parents. This entire book is completely powered by the long-term implications of an affair and my dad's addiction to alcohol. Satan gets to steal and rob future unborn generations of their happiness, holiness, and joy in Jesus just by making it look appealing to unwind.

Maybe you are thinking that you are doing alright because none of what I mentioned applies to you. It doesn't apply to me, either. But don't get too much of an ego just yet. The devil can't make me bad, so instead, he makes me busy. That's right. He is a thief, and he steals my time! Maybe he steals your time, too. He cleverly tricks me into believing that if I am busy, I am productive. I thrive on thinking I am productive, and so I will often load my proverbial plate with work and activities until I have no room for anything else. When I don't have time to spend with Jesus or read my Bible, I will often explain it away with my schedule. I make an excuse instead of just repenting as

I should. My lack of prayer leads to a short temper with my kids and husband. My full schedule leaves little time to tend to the things at my house, which leads to anger and frustration. The devil will have me yelling at everyone and causing chaos and tension in my home just because I wanted to feel productive. See how clever he can be? The point is, until Jesus gets you in His camp and begins to train your heart to see things from a new perspective, the devil will have you out there acting like a fool.

He will have you wrecking relationships, sowing division, and making a mockery of the Word of God with every action you take. The worst part is that he will convince you that you oversee your life and your destiny. He is so cunning that he will have you taking ownership of his evil plans by making you feel like the master of your own destiny. Meanwhile, your life is nothing more than a display of ventriloquism. He will be your master, pulling the strings while you are nothing more than an unsuspecting puppet in his demonic schemes. What an annoying jerk.

Make no mistake about it. On the day you give your life to Christ, Satan dispatches every demon in hell to bring a fight to

CHAPTER 8: FREEDOM FIGHTER

your doorstep. His battle plan changes because he has lost a soul that he desperately wanted to take to hell with him. He also lost a warrior in his evil army, and that is a monumental threat to him. He doesn't want you out there working for the kingdom of God and experiencing joy! He wants to make it hard on you. So hard that you decide to call it quits. Unless you know your enemy and what you need to do to combat his schemes, he will begin to reclaim ground in your life. God writes your name down in the Lamb's Book of Life and marks you with his seal! You are *his child.* From the day of your salvation, God begins a new work in you, and this knowledge brings forth an expectant heart. New believers are filled with joy and hope about the thing to come! The devil, seeking whom he may devour, cleverly sneaks in and begins the process of trying to snuff out your light. The devil doesn't want one person to follow Christ. The devil, once a beautiful angel, was thrown out of heaven because of his jealousy and great pride. Scripture says:

> "How you have fallen from heaven, morning star, son of the dawn! You have been cast down to the earth, you who once laid low the nations! You said in your heart, "I will ascend to the heavens; I will raise

> my throne above the stars of God; I will sit enthroned on the mount of assembly, on the utmost heights of Mount Zaphon. I will ascend above the tops of the clouds; I will make myself like the Most High."
>
> ISAIAH 14:12–14

The devil became jealous of God and wanted to reign over Him. Some theologians think that the devil was envious of Jesus sitting at the right hand of the Father and thought He deserved the position. They claim that when God said to Jesus, **"Let us make man in our image, after our likeness"** (Genesis 1:26), the devil's envy grew out of control because of his great pride. The Bible says that Lucifer was beautiful.

Ezekiel 28:17: **"Your heart was proud because of your beauty; you corrupted your wisdom for the sake of your splendor. I cast you to the ground; I exposed you before kings, to feast their eyes on you."** His beauty might have led him to believe that God should have made man after his image and not that of Jesus. While I certainly think that is a plausible argument, I think I am going to wait to get to Heaven and ask God what is was that pushed the devil into the sin that got him evicted. One thing we know for sure is that Satan was kicked out of Heaven and declared an enemy of God. Jesus himself makes reference to the fall of Satan in the book of Luke.

> He replied, "I saw Satan fall like lightning from heaven. I have given you authority to trample on snakes and scorpions and to overcome all the power of the enemy; nothing will harm you. However, do not rejoice that the spirits submit to you, but rejoice that your names are written in heaven."
>
> LUKE 10:18–20

I don't think people truly understand the spiritual warfare that takes place for the believer. Angels and demons are engaged in a constant war that rages in the spiritual realm. The fighting is intense because the prize is your soul. The devil doesn't want anyone to reach heaven or experience the joy that comes with serving Jesus. He wants to drag as many souls to hell with him as possible. The devil is full of pride and jealousy. This is why he got kicked out of heaven in the first place.

Hindsight is 20/20; isn't that what they say? For years, I let the devil defeat me. I believed the lies that were written on my heart like the gospel. I spoke death and defeat over myself on more than one occasion. Regretfully, I didn't realize the freedom that comes with serving God, and I was needlessly living in torment. Satan still tries to invade my mind from time to time, but now I am battle-ready! When I feel his arrows start to penetrate my heart and mind, I put up my shield *and* quickly draw my sword! The sword makes all the difference.

I once heard a little country preacher give one of the most powerful analogies of serving God that I have ever heard. He likened men and women of God to soldiers in the army. He asked the church to think about the United States Army and what they do when they go to work every day. He went on to explain that a soldier's job is to protect the nation at all costs. As such, they are either in a war or training for war at all times! If a soldier isn't fighting in a war, they are sharpening their skills. A soldier in the army of the Lord is just the same! We should no sooner get out of one battle than we begin preparing for another! How do we prepare for battle? Just like our military, we sharpen our skills. We study and learn how to use our weapons! The more I thought about this little sermon, the more profound it became.

CHAPTER 8: FREEDOM FIGHTER

If you study the Word of God, we truly are soldiers in the army of the Lord. God outlines the armor of God in Ephesians 6:10–18. We have the belt of truth, the breastplate of righteousness, the helmet of salvation, the shield of faith, our feet fitted with readiness, and our sword of the Spirit, the Word of God. It is interesting to me that of all of the armor God tells us to wear, there is only one offensive weapon. The rest of the pieces of armor are defensive weapons. We can shield ourselves from the darts of the enemy by wearing all that God has told us to put on. We can hunker down and deflect Satan all day, every day, but we can't make him retreat until we pick up our weapon and fight! The Word of God is the weapon of choice! If you want to fight back and send your enemy running, you *must* know the Word of God! Imagine hunkering down, hiding behind your shield. Carrying around the weight of the protection of the breastplate, the helmet, the belt, the shoes is heavy. You will get worn out from carrying it day after day just trying to deflect the lies of the enemy. I think that many people, including myself, forget to draw their swords, and so they are completely exhausted from one moment to the next. I got battle-weary and wanted to raise the white flag of defeat so many times. I did not understand why I could never seem to get the devil to leave my mind alone! Did God not care if I was getting tormented? Was God able to do it for others but not for me? Was I really sinful and unsaved and fooling myself? Questions like this taunted me until, one day, the Lord told me to pick up my sword and stand firm against the devil. When I picked it up, I became a worthy adversary! For the first time in my life, I felt the devil retreat and flee from my mind. It was a glorious revelation to know that God didn't leave me. He was waiting for me to realize the power He gave me on the day I became His! When I stood up and pointed my sword of the Spirit at the throat of the enemy, I became a threat. Satan knows how powerful the Word is, and he can't withstand the truth that it brings. The Word is our weapon, and our weapon never fails.

When Satan sends troublesome thoughts our way, God's Word tells us how to fight. In 2 Corinthians 10:5, God tells us: **"We demolish arguments and every pretension that sets itself up against the knowledge of God, and we take captive every thought to make to make it obedient to Christ."**

My mistake was not taking intrusive thoughts captive and making them obedient to the Word of God immediately. I let them linger and fed them until they grew into a monster that felt too big to capture. If you are guilty of feeding your demons instead of taking them captive, then it's time for you to pick up your sword and cut them down at the source.

"Put on the whole armor of God, that you may be able to stand against the schemes of the devil" (Ephesians 6:11).

The whole armor of God includes the sword as your weapon. If you use everything else and fail to use the sword, you won't be able to *stand* against the devil. You will be crouching down and just fighting off the blows.

> "Be strong and very courageous. Be careful to obey all the law my servant Moses gave you; do not turn from it to the right or to the left, that you may be successful wherever you go. Keep this Book of Law always on your lips; meditate on it day and night, so that you may be careful to do everything written in it. Then you will be prosperous and successful."
>
> JOSHUA 1:7–8

God very plainly tells us that if we want to be prosperous and successful in this life, we have to study and know His Word for ourselves. Not only that, but we also have to obey His laws and commands. God is gracious to us, and He lovingly tells us things over and over again throughout the scripture. In Joshua, God tells us to study the Word and think about it all the time so that we can obey God's laws. In Ephesians, God tells us to put on our armor of God and fight the lies of the enemy with His Word. The Word is living and is the absolute truth. An intimate understanding of the Scripture is the only way we conquer the battlefield of our minds and walk in victory.

This sounds easy enough, but how do we actually put this into practice? Here is one way I use the Word of God in my own life when I am fighting the devil.

The devil tells me: "You are wasting your potential. You should have been so much more successful by now."

I tell the devil what God says: **"And I am certain that God, who began the good work in me, will continue His work until it is finally finished on the day when Christ Jesus returns"** (Philippians 1:6).

Do you see how Satan's lie was contradicted by God's truth? The devil would have me believe that I have run out of time to be successful in my life, in my ministry, etc. God's Word tells me that this can't be true because God is faithful to finish what He starts in me. I take my thoughts captive and make them obedient to Christ when I can combat them with divine truth. The truth makes the devil retreat.

The devil whispers: "Being a stay-at-home mother is so unrewarding. You have no real talent and abilities."

I tell the devil what God says: **"My children arise and call me blessed. My husband also, he praises me. Many women have done excellently, but I surpass them all"** (Proverbs 31:28–29).

God's Word promises that if I am serving Him wholeheartedly, my husband and children will be blessed for it. They will honor me and praise me for being an excellent mother and wife. Serving God wholeheartedly means that you are a woman who is desperately seeking God despite your failures.

The devil will say, "You are so ugly. You better get botox and fillers and work out all the time so you can stay attractive."

I tell the devil what God says, **"I will be known for the beauty that comes from within, the unfading beauty of a gentle and quiet spirit, which is so precious to God"** (1 Peter 3:4).

The devil says, "God doesn't really love you, or He wouldn't let you go through all these horrible things."

I tell the devil what God says, **"And we know that in all things God works together for the good of those who love Him, who have been called according to His purpose"** (Romans 8:28).

The devil says, "You are too broken to fix. You should kill yourself and do the world a favor."

I tell the devil what God says, **"The Lord is close to the broken-hearted and saves those who are crushed in spirit"** (Psalm 34:18).

I don't let the enemy get a foothold in my life anymore because I know that the Word of God will always combat his lies. I spend time reading the Bible each day so that I personally know what God's Word says and can put the devil in his place with it. Whatever lies the enemy is telling you today, just know that God's Word will provide you with the truth you need to combat it. Find the antidote to the devil's poison in Scripture and commit to memorizing it. Write it on an index card. Tape it to your mirror. Carry it with you in the car. Do whatever you need to do to write in on your heart and silence your enemy.

CHAPTER 9:
The Keys to the Kingdom

The single most crippling fear that has hindered my journey to joy and righteousness has been my fear of blind faith. When you wholeheartedly serve God, He expects that you trust Him completely. He wants us to have faith that he is who he says he is and is able to do what he promises. Faith in him is the single most important act of service you can give him because, without it, you will never be obedient to him. James 2:26 says, **"Faith without works is dead."** The "works" he is referring to are the different acts of obedience that he will ask us to complete without question. I have found that it is in those works that God answers the prayers of His people that He draws the unbeliever closer to Him and completes His perfect will on this earth. A single act of obedience by a child of God could be the way God chooses to leave the ninety-one and rescue the one. When you look at it like that, it is easy to see why God requires trust and obedience from His children.

The trouble that women like you and I face is that we have been near fatally wounded by someone we love betraying our trust. And when you have grown up learning that those you trust will ultimately hurt you, trusting someone you have never *seen* becomes quite the task. Nevertheless, God wants our complete trust and obedience, so we have to find a way to overcome and heal the wounds of the flesh.

Before we go any further, I want to give you a practical example of trust and obedience in action. When my husband got out of the army and we moved back to our hometown, we didn't have a lot of money. In fact, our account was overdrawn more often than not. I had created a delicate cycle of paying bills that avoided a disconnect but also tacked on a late fee while also leaving enough to buy groceries. We had both grown up poor, so the struggle wasn't new for us, but having to learn to work the system to keep the lights on was difficult to learn as an adult.

We had a toddler when he got out of the army, and it wasn't long after that God blessed us with a daughter. I was a teacher, and my husband was working at a major home improvement chain, so we didn't have enough money to make ends meet, but we also didn't qualify for any help through government programs. In addition to learning how to work the due dates and late fees in a way that kept the lights on, we also saved every single piece of change we found for unexpected expenses. I would often take the change jar to the grocery store and put it in the change machine so I could go inside and buy what we needed.

One month, our infant daughter became so sick that she was in the hospital for several days. I had already used all of my sick days with our toddler during the fall, so I had no paid days left for this unexpected event. I missed about ten days of work with no pay, and by the time we got discharged from the hospital, we were in a dire financial situation. We needed groceries and formula, but we didn't have a dime in our checking account, so I loaded up my ole faithful change bucket, which was about halfway full, and went to the grocery store. As I was walking in, I saw a woman who worked as a teacher's aide in the school I taught at. Her autistic son was in my class, and so she and I had spoken several times, but we weren't what I would call good friends. I say this only to tell you that I didn't know her well enough to know her financial situation or even if she had a spouse. I waved hello and went on to the change machine when I had a strange thought. I thought, *You should give this money to her when you change it in.* I immediately pushed it out of my mind because I *needed* that money and couldn't go home empty-handed. As the change ticked through the counter, the thought became louder in my mind.

I had been praying and drawing closer to the Lord in my home life, but up until this day, I don't ever remember hearing a specific direction from the Lord. To be completely honest, I didn't know it was the Lord right away because I wasn't used to having the Lord impress things on my heart. I also didn't audibly hear His voice. It was a soft, gentle thought that became louder and more urgent as the minutes passed by. I was so conflicted at first because I knew that I needed the money, and it wasn't clear to me right away that God would provide for my needs if I was obedient to Him. I was still young in my faith and knowledge of the Lord, and so I couldn't begin to fathom the full picture of the way He would bless our lives with this one simple act of obedience. I also worried that I would offend her by giving her money. I didn't know her well enough to know how she would respond to the gesture, and I would have been mortified if she had been offended. Ultimately, the thought in my mind became so persistent that I realized God must be wanting me to do it. I gave her the money, and she graciously accepted it. It was actually a rather quick interaction. I grabbed what I absolutely had to have and hoped that my overdraft protection plan would allow the payment to go through at the register. As I was leaving the store, the woman stopped me. She looked equal parts bewildered and amazed. She told me that she couldn't believe that the money I had given her was almost the exact amount of what she needed. She went on to tell me that she needed something for her son that she didn't really have the money to buy. She was praying that the Lord would help her financial situation and provide, and then I walked up to her and gave her money, and the amount wound up being just what she needed!

The Lord used the one simple act of obedience to strengthen her faith and answer the prayer that she had been praying. It was also such an encouragement to me! I was in awe that God had A) spoken to me directly and B) answered someone's prayer through my act of obedience. I didn't feel worthy of either of those things, so it was shocking to know that He had chosen me to be the vessel He used that day and in that way. I didn't know how God would provide for my family if I gave the money away, and I had a great trust issue that made me skeptical that God would come through for us. That probably sounds awful to say, but it is true nonetheless. I was new in my faith and still had *tons* of healing to do about my trust issues. I could have taken care of me and my family that day, but I am so thankful that my heart was tender enough to listen.

As awesome as the answer to her prayer is, that's not where this story ended for me. I still had the issue of the overdrawn account. I prayed that the Lord would help us financially and left it at that. Of course, I worried and obsessed all night about how I was going to get money to put into our checking account to cover the amount and the overdraft fee because worrying is what I did best. The next morning, I got ready and went to work, and on my planning period, I checked my teacher mailbox in the front office. I found a white envelope stuffed inside with my name on it. Inside, I found a note wrapped around some money. The note was just a few short sentences, but it had me standing there at my mailbox, bawling like a baby. It read something like this:

"I know you had to take days without pay when your daughter was sick. That happened to me when my kids were young, and I know how hard it can be. I took up a collection for you, and even though it's not much, I hope it helps you and your family a little!"

It was triple the amount I had given the woman the day before! I was *so amazed* that I wanted to tell anyone who would listen about what the Lord had done. It activated something inside of me that I had never felt before. I was on *fire* for the Lord from that point forward. I wanted to hear Him talk to me; I desperately wanted to obey! Not because of what He had done for me financially but because I wanted to be a willing vessel that the Lord used to work! I had never seen such an intricate plan work out like that in all my life, and I was more sure than ever that there was a God who loved me and wanted good and not harm for me.

This one act of obedience, as difficult as it was, was a catalyst for our future. The more time I spent in the presence of the Lord, the clearer His voice became! If God told me to go, I went. If God told me to give, I gave. If God told me to speak, I spoke. And each time I obeyed Him, He allowed me to witness His hand at work. I was secretive and careful about my giving so that only God knew what we had done. What is done in secret, God is faithful to bless in public, and that is what happened to us. Our marriage began to strengthen and transform. The favor of the Lord gave my husband a job that allowed our finances to be blessed. The favor of the Lord allowed me to begin my journey of staying at home with my kids and ultimately heal my heart from the pain of a broken childhood.

Now feels like a good time to press pause and revisit how hard it is for someone who feels broken and abused to trust God. The story I just told you sounds like it was a breeze to walk through, but that's because I just gave you the encouraging highlight reel. As you know, there were many dark, turbulent times in my journey that caused me to almost give up. At the root of all my issues were broken trust and a broken heart that I experienced at such a young age. I'm sure that many of you reading this now have also dealt with things that make you question if there is a loving God at all. If He is loving and all-knowing, why would He allow so many people, especially children, to go through the things that we do? I will admit, I have meditated on this question often, always searching for a clear and concise answer.

I have a little notebook that I keep beside my Bible. At the top of different pages, I have different topics that I would like to learn more about, and as I read something relevant to it in my Bible, I write the Scripture under that topic. One of the pages says, "Why would God allow the innocent to suffer?"

For those struggling with trust or wondering if God is even real, this answer to this question is of the highest concern. The ones who struggle with trust issues are the ones who have had our trust violated so intimately that it is hard to reconcile how we can fully trust a God who allowed those things to happen. I have found that if we are faithful to ask God what perplexes our souls, He is faithful to lead us to the answers that He has written in His Word.

The short answer is that there is not a short answer to this question. Instead, we have to be able to see how different scriptures in the Bible fit together to reveal the answers to the most puzzling question. I don't think there is a one-size-fits-all answer, either. I think it serves the body of believers well to pray that God would reveal to you why you had to deal with certain circumstances and then stay rooted in the study of His Word. I can tell you without a shadow of a doubt that God is faithful to answer you and fully satisfy what you have been longing for. For the purposes of this book, I am going to provide you with two examples of trust and obedience that were difficult and painful for the people involved but ultimately led them to a faith in God's purposes coming to pass. My desire is that these examples of great faith and obedience might serve as a launching pad for your own prayer and study.

My life was completely changed by the single act of adultery that my father committed. That one single desire, when acted upon, was the first domino in a series of events that would lead me to dangerous alcohol use and sexual immorality as a young woman and later give way to such low self-esteem that I would struggle with darkness and depression for many years. As a young girl, I was violated and exposed to things that no child should have to be exposed to. Later, I did things that weren't meant for anyone, let alone a teenage girl. Ultimately, the question I had to face was this: If God loves me, why didn't He rescue me when I was the hurting little girl?

First, let's look at the example God gives us in the Book of Job. Job has admittedly always been a hard book for me to read because it's hard to understand why God would choose to cause a righteous man to suffer unnecessarily. It wasn't until reading it again this year that God showed me how much there is to learn about His nature in the Book of Job.

The first thing to consider when studying Job is that although it is hard to read what Job went through, God, the author and finisher of all things, was privy to the end of Job's life. He knew that Job would not die destitute and broken-hearted. He would not leave His faithful servant in that state. He knew that the latter part of his life would be greater than the first! Where we see it part, God sees in full. God orders the steps of the righteous.

"And we know that in all things God works for the good of those who love him, who have been called according to his purpose" (Romans 8:28).

For Job, "all things" referred to the great test that he experienced. For us, "all things" refers to the pain and suffering that we have experienced at the hand of others and maybe even because of our own choices and actions. But God, knowing that His Word is absolute, knew that He worked all things for the good of Job and that Job would experience joy and happiness again. He also knows the plans He has for you and me, friend. He knows that He will work everything out for our good *if* we love Him.

I know what you're thinking. But what about Job's children? This has always been a struggle for me. Why did he have to experience the heartache of losing his children? For this, I lean on Scripture, and it helps me understand. First, we know that Job was a righteous man. When Satan approached God and said he was roaming the earth looking back and forth on it, God immediately thought of Job. Not because God wanted to bring punishment on Job but because He knew how much Job loved Him! Think on that a minute. Of all the people on earth, God chose Job to remind Satan that God has ultimate authority. What an honor it was for Job to be hand-picked by God to go up against Satan! He knew that Satan would approach Him and try and entice Him into allowing evil to befall Job, so God had been preparing Job for this very test. God, being God, also knew that He needed to provide an example for future generations seeking the very answers we are seeking today. He gave us a stark example of a good person suffering for no obvious reason so that we could draw wisdom, knowledge, and encouragement from in the life of Job.

Let's have a quick Q and A of biblical trivia.

Q: What does the Bible say about a righteous man?

A: "The prayers of a righteous man availeth much" (James 5:16).

Q: What does the Bible say happens when you raise a child in the knowledge of the Lord?

A: "Train up a child in the way he should go, and when he is old he will not depart from it" (Proverbs 22:6).

Q: *Which is better for those who love God, to live or to die?*

A: "For to me, to live is Christ and to die is gain" (Philippians 1:21).

Q: *Can you pray protection for your children so that Satan can't touch them?*

A: "Have you not put a hedge around him and his household and everything he has?" (Job 1:10)

Job was a righteous man that prayed for his children. In Job 1:4–5, it says:

> "His sons used to hold feasts in their homes on their birthdays, and they would invite their three sisters to eat and drink with them. When a period of feasting had run its course, Job would make arrangements for them to be purified. Early in the morning he would

> sacrifice a burnt offering for each of them, thinking, 'Perhaps my children have sinned and cursed God in their hearts.' This was Job's regular custom."

So we know he prayed for his children. Further, when Satan is speaking to God about Job, he says, "Does Job fear for nothing? Have you not put a hedge around him and his household and everything he has?" God included this very important detail to show us that our prayers today can literally place protection from Satan's attacks on our children but also to show us that Job had covered his children in prayer.

Because I know what scripture promises, I can see that Job's prayers were effective because he was righteous. As such, I can be confident that he trained his children up in the knowledge of the Lord, and although it doesn't explicitly say it, I can be sure that each child was given the opportunity to know the Lord before their death. Later, in the Book of Philippians, the Bible assures me that when you know God, death is actually better than life because, in death, you get to your eternal home. Job would momentarily experience grief of earth, but because of God's promises, he can be sure of his children's eternal home.

Looking at Job's life shows me several things about my own pain. First, I had parents who, at times, tried to teach me about God, but my dad was not a righteous man. He did not pray for a hedge of protection around his children and family. God demonstrates to us that if you are not praying a hedge of protection around your family as a righteous man or woman of God, then Satan can launch a full-on assault against them. This is how many of us get wounded as children. Evil exists on this earth. That is an unfortunate fact. Without parents or loved ones interceding for children, evil things happen to children because the devil has full access to them. My father was not a righteous man, and because he was determined to live in the flesh, he gave the devil complete access to my sister and I. That was not God's fault. The blame there lies on my father, the leader of our household.

Job's life also reminds us that even when bad things happen to good people, God is faithful to work them out on our behalf. Sometimes, there is no logical reason that explains why bad things happen to us. Maybe you were raised by righteous parents who prayed for you and lived for God, but bad things still happened to you that left you hurt and broken. Job did not bring evil on himself; he was on the receiving end of terrible circumstances. Because we know this about Job, we can be assured that even when things don't make sense to our natural minds, we can trust that God will work everything out for our good if we will remain steadfast and faithful to Him. Job trusted and obeyed God even though things didn't make sense to him. As a result, God blessed him.

Finally, we can look to the Israelites and learn a lesson on suffering from them. The Israelites brought suffering upon themselves by their constant disobedience and unbelief. God led them out of bondage and told them they were to inherit the land flowing with milk and honey (Exodus 3:8). When they sent the twelve men to spy on the current inhabitants of the land, they became discouraged and convinced that they could not defeat them. The unbelief was in direct contrast to what God had said was going to happen. They could not trust God to provide them victory even though God had just faithfully led them out of captivity. As a result of their disobedience and unbelief, they wandered the desert for forty years. The unbelieving generation died off, and the new generation inhabited the promised land just as God said. The children born during the forty years were innocent, but because of their parent's decisions, they were forced to bear the consequence as well. What I find so encouraging is that the very generation that suffered as a result of their parents' unbelief was the very generation that decided to trust God and see! They got to enter the promised land, and God blessed them abundantly! We can also choose to be the generation of people that proudly proclaims victory! We don't have to walk in the rebellious footsteps of our parents. Instead, we can be like the generation that inhabited the land despite what their older generation did! Bitter or better. That's the choice.

Hebrews 3:7–19 is a warning against unbelief.

> So, as the Holy Spirit says:
>
> "Today if you hear his voice, do not harden your hearts as you did in the rebellion, during times of testing in the wilderness, where your ancestors tested and tried me, though for forty years they saw what I did. That is why I was angry with that generation; I said, 'Their hearts are always going astray, and they have not known my ways.' So I declared an oath in my anger, 'They shall never enter my rest.'"
>
> See to it, brothers and sisters, that none of you has

> a sinful, unbelieving heart that turns away from the living God. But encourage one another daily, as long as it is called "today," so that none of you may be hardened by sin's deceitfulness. We have come to share in Christ, if indeed we hold our original conviction firmly to the very end. As has just been said:
>
> "Today, if you hear his voice, do not harden your hearts as you did in the rebellion."
>
> Who were they who heard and rebelled? Were they not all those Moses led out of Egypt? And with whom was he angry for forty years? Was it not with those who sinned, whose bodies perished in the wilderness? And to whom did God swear that they would never enter into his rest if not to those who disobeyed? So we see that they were not able to enter, because of their unbelief.

Without faith, it is impossible to please God (Hebrews 11:6). Central to faith is trust. The devil attacks our trust issues and renders us incapable of obeying God. If you want to be victorious, I urge you to step out of the boat, step away from the raging storm that has been your life, and just reach for Jesus. Return to your childlike nature and willfully trust that your Father who loves you knows what is best for you today. He won't let you down, and you'll never be disappointed.

CHAPTER 10:
Say Whaaaattt?

We've walked through our hurt together. We've talked about salvation and the redeeming power of the blood. We've looked in the mirror and examined the sins that keep us bound up in shackles and chains. We've learned what it means to be a captive of war and also what it looks like to go to war as a soldier in the army of the Lord. We've talked about faith and obedience. We've actually talked about an awful lot. The only thing left to talk about now is our words. How's that for irony?

I often pray, "Lord, if she doesn't have anything nice to say, muzzle her mouth!" That might not sound like the most Christian prayer you've ever heard, but I don't want anyone speaking slander against me and giving the devil anything to use against me later. I also have to remind myself that I might need to muzzle my own mouth from time to time. You probably do, too. Our words have power! Did you know that the devil cannot hear the thoughts you think and only operates against you by hearing the words that you speak? It's true! Satan is not privy to your inner man. Only God searches the heart. The devil spends his time roaming the earth, seeking whom he may devour. He devours the people that give him the most to chew on.

"Life and death are in the power of the tongue, and those who love it will eat its fruit" (Proverbs 18:21).

Women who walk in the authority and victory of Christ are women who freely operate in the fruits of the Spirit. Those fruits are love, joy, peace, patience, kindness, goodness, faithfulness, gentleness, and self-control. Self-control is the ribbon that ties the fruits together in a nice little package. If self-control of the tongue is lacking, the fruits of the Spirit won't be effective or useful to the body of Christ. I'll be the first to admit that self-control is sometimes hard for me and is the area I struggle with the most. I value justice and want the scales of life to be as balanced as possible. When I don't feel like people are operating on a fair scale, I get hot-headed and catch myself speaking before I think things through. This never ends well for me. It's hard to show love, joy, peace, and so on when you are telling someone off. Truth be told, sometimes I gossip, too. Satan uses what I say against a brother or sister as ammunition. One moment of weakness where you lash out in anger can cause months of heartache and distraction. One whisper to another can damage a reputation and spread like wildfire, killing the witness of another. Satan loves it when we don't exercise self-control of the tongue.

The words that we speak are also a representation of what is in our hearts. Jesus had some harsh words for those listening to Him in Matthew 12:33–35:

> "You brood of vipers, how can you who are evil say anything good? For the mouth speaks what the heart is full of. A good man brings good things out of the good stored up in him, and an evil man brings evil things out of the evil stored up in him."

Jesus is clear in His message. If you speak garbage, your heart is full of garbage. If you speak hateful talk, your heart is full of hate. If you speak words that tear down, your heart is full of contempt. The opposite is also true. If you speak words of life over someone, the message of your heart tells a different story. It's safe to say that our heart is revealed by the words that come out of our mouths. Can shifting our thought process and our subsequent words help us develop the fruit of the spirit? Absolutely! With God's wisdom, we can begin to understand why it is so important that we watch our words.

God spoke creation into existence. It's hard for me to even grasp, but He literally spoke words and called creation into existence. If God, in His supernatural holiness, created you and me in His image and likeness, it only makes sense that we can also speak declarations over ourselves and our families. Words matter to God. So, it begs the question. How's your vocabulary?

Did you know that God told Moses what He calls Himself in Exodus chapter 3? I find that fascinating. It is generally known that God's name is YAHWEH. But God also calls Himself another name when speaking to Moses. In Exodus chapter 3, Moses has an encounter with God at the burning bush. Here, God instructs Moses to go to Pharaoh and bring the Israelites out of Egypt. A couple of noteworthy things happen during this encounter.

The first thing Moses did was question God. What a totally obnoxiously human thing to do. Moses didn't believe in himself enough to think he was worthy of such a holy task. He was sure that somehow God had chosen the wrong person. There's

CHAPTER 10: SAY WHAAATTT?

a whole sermon wrapped up in that thought process, but how often do we hinder our own God-given purpose by thinking just like Moses did here? When God told Moses to go, he replied with, "Who am I that I should go to Pharoah and bring the Israelites out of Egypt?"

God answered him, "I will be with you. And this will be the sign to you that it is I who have sent you: when you have brought the people out of Egypt, you will worship God on this mountain."

Notice that God didn't tell Moses how qualified he was or shower him with positive affirmations about himself to make him feel more capable. Instead, He referred Moses back to him! In essence, God said for Moses to quit thinking it had anything to do with him and focus on God. God doesn't look for the qualified; He looks for the willing! Whatever God wants to use you to do, remember that it has never been about you. If you don't or won't do it, God will find someone who will!

Moses, appearing to still doubt God, continues to use his words to call God's instructions into question.

Moses said to God, "Suppose I go to the Israelites and say to them, 'The God of the Fathers has sent me to you, and they ask me, 'What's his name?' Then what should I tell them?"

God answered Moses in the most beautiful way. He said to him, "*I am who I am*. This is what you are to say to the Israelites: *I am* has sent me to you. This is My name forever, the name you shall call Me from generation to generation." God names Himself "I am." It's interesting to note that another Hebrew translation of *I am* is "I will be." It is derived from the Hebrew word *ehyeh*.

Now, bear with me just a minute as we unpack something that completely blew my mind the first time I heard it. Keep in mind that in Proverbs 18:21, God tells us that the power of life and death is in the tongue. Did He mean that figuratively or quite literally? Well, let's do a little wordplay.

Like Moses, we constantly think of and our thoughts usually surround ourselves. That's not necessarily a bad thing, but it can certainly be a hindrance to our growth if we aren't aware of the power that lies within how we speak. Every woman I know begins almost every sentence with the following two words, "I am…"

CHAPTER 10: SAY WHAAATTT?

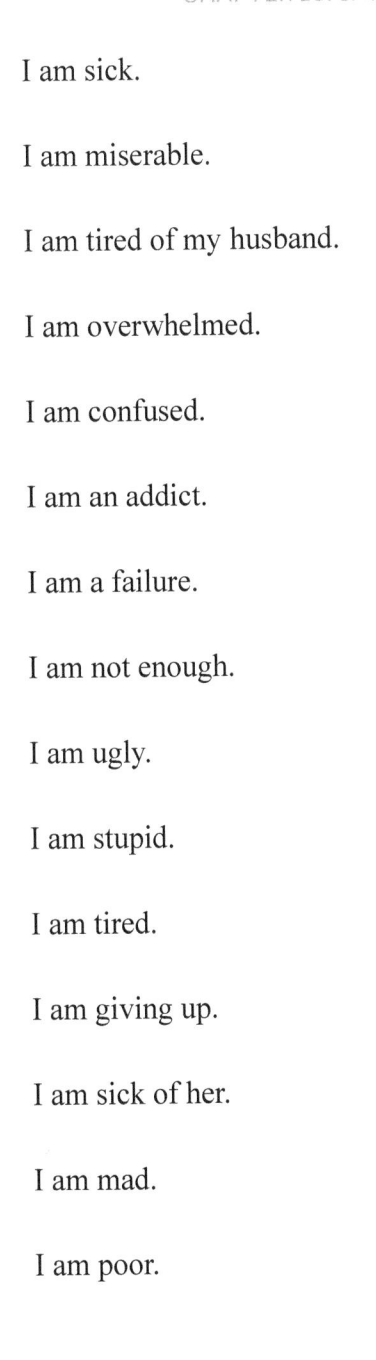

I am sick.

I am miserable.

I am tired of my husband.

I am overwhelmed.

I am confused.

I am an addict.

I am a failure.

I am not enough.

I am ugly.

I am stupid.

I am tired.

I am giving up.

I am sick of her.

I am mad.

I am poor.

I am broken.

I am unsatisfied.

I am not content.

I am never going to measure up.

I am not the right one for this task.

I am incapable.

I am worthless.

We are made in the likeness of God, and we begin every single sentence about ourselves with the name that God chose to call Himself in the burning bush. Is that a coincidence? You already know how I feel about coincidences when it comes to God. There is no such thing. Let's take those sentences that we speak over ourselves on a daily basis and apply them to the one we are made to resemble and see how that sounds.

God is sick.

God is miserable.

CHAPTER 10: SAY WHAAATTT?

God is tired of my husband.

God is overwhelmed.

God is confused.

God is worthless.

God is incapable.

God is not the right one for this task.

You get the idea. It feels sacrilegious to speak any of those sentences about God. But sister, you and I were created in His very likeness, and that's exactly how we talk about ourselves every single day. He sent His Son to die for us. His son willingly laid down His life for us. I'm sure He doesn't take too kindly to hearing us speak declarations of death over ourselves. Do you hear what I am telling you? You might be overwhelmed. You might be tired of your husband. You might be sick. But you don't have to speak it into existence! Keep that to yourself, and don't give the devil an ounce of ammunition. If you know life and death are in the power of the tongue and you continue to speak negatively, then I just don't know what to tell you.

You can be saved, you can be baptized, you can be the worship leader of your church, you can be all the things, but if you don't have control of your words, you will never walk into the victory and authority that God has given you.

My family always tells my husband and me that we could fall into a pile of poop and sit up smelling like roses. It's a compliment, I guess, but what they are really saying is that they can't believe that even when bad things happen to us, we always come out better than we were before. And it's true. The favor of the Lord has rested heavily on our family. We definitely don't deserve it. We sin and fall short of the glory of God every single day of our lives. But we are faithful to repent quickly and speak life even when choosing to speak death would be easier. I've walked around hospital rooms and rebuked the devil and spoken life into my sick children. I've raised my hands in worship as I did laps around the hospital bed, praising God for the wonder-working power of His healing hand even though my insides were shaking with fear! I don't give the devil a syllable that sounds like defeat, and neither does my husband. We've praised when we wanted to scream. We've worshipped when the very fiber of our existence told us to worry.

We made a conscious decision that we would speak life even if the natural order of things looked like death. In our finances, in our marriage, and in our home. It has made all the difference. We didn't always do this, but once we began trusting God, obeying Him, and speaking life, our lives became living testimonies to the goodness of God.

Learning to do this took work. *Lots of work.* We had to retrain our thought patterns so we didn't focus on the negative. Each of us has two natures that dwell within us, begging to be fed. It's the *spirit* versus the *flesh* every single time. If I yield to the flesh, negativity, confusion, and chaos rule my heart, and out of the heart, the mouth speaks. If I feed my spirit and starve my flesh, my central focus becomes God. If my mind is on Him, my heart will be too. My thought patterns and language will reflect a life focused on the spirit.

> "Those who live according to the flesh have their minds set on what the flesh desires; but those who live in accordance with the Spirit have their minds set on what their spirit desires. The mind governed by the flesh is death, but the mind governed by the spirit is life and peace. The mind governed by the

> flesh is hostile to God, it does not submit to God's law, nor can it do so. Those who are in the realm of the flesh cannot praise God."
>
> ROMANS 8:5–8

Not only is speaking negatively not productive, it displeases God! I don't want to yield to the flesh. I want my thoughts, words, and actions to be pleasing to God because I love Him and because I want to live a life of peace. It is possible to get to a place where you are so focused on God that when bad things happen or unfortunate circumstances arise, your thoughts are disrupted with lies from the enemy. If you can get to a place where your heart is guarded and focused on God, you will find victory and authority overflowing and spilling into all areas of your life.

Some practical ways that I have found that help me stay focused on the spirit involve words! If I am feeling negative, I turn on some worship music and praise my way out of a negative mood. If I am feeling confused, I remember that the truth lies in the Scripture, and I read my Bible until God gives me peace. If I am sad or mad and want to tell someone what I think about them, I talk to God instead. I pray that God would give me a gentle heart as well as help me to see the situation through His eyes. I regularly repent of my sins, and I call them out to God. This helps me to remember that I don't belong on a high horse judging anyone else. I allow God to correct me even when it's painful. I draw from my own experience as a parent and remember that a parent disciplines a child because of their great love for them, not for the punishment. I remain disciplined in my worship. I don't regularly listen to music that would make me want to go to "da club" (because I used to love doing that), and I don't go places where I am tempted to gossip or otherwise sin. I have learned to bridle my tongue by practicing the pause. I still get irate quite frequently, and I like to joke that I am from the "south side" of the kingdom where we throw hands, but alas, I am a forty-two-year-old mother who hasn't thrown hands since freshman year. When I am angered, I try my best to spend time thinking and in prayer and even sleep on it before I react. My responses are always more controlled when I practice the pause. These small acts, applied to my life on a consistent basis, have helped me to cultivate the fruit of the spirit known as self-control. And just like I said earlier, self-control ties the rest of the fruits together and makes for a meaningful, joyful, and victorious life!

You were made in God's image!

You were made for peace that passes understanding!

You were made to walk in righteousness!

You were made for authority over the principalities and rulers of darkness!

You were made for victory over the enemy!

You were made for joy everlasting!

You were made in His image…

And,

> "About the son he says, Your throne, O God, will last forever and ever; a scepter of justice will be the scepter of your kingdom. You were made for righteousness and hated wickedness; therefore God, your God, has set you above your companions by anointing you with the oil of joy."
>
> **HEBREWS 1:9**

And all the King's daughters said, "Amen."

Printed in the USA
CPSIA information can be obtained
at www.ICGtesting.com
LVHW080557290124
769933LV00012B/280